Dedicated to all those grappling with this debilitating and little understood condition.

All proceeds from the sale of this book will go ME / CFS charities in the UK.

Preface

We are very fortunate to have two wonderful children, a close-knit extended family and a comfortable lifestyle. Born in 2001, Jessica was a lively and confident young child who shared a very special and close relationship with her brother, born three years later. We enjoyed many happy family events: ten years of holidays in France with my parents, wonderful times in the Cotswolds with my husband's family, regular weekends away with friends and a multitude of kiddie activities to give our children a wide exposure to the potential opportunities around them. Both enjoyed acting, singing and dancing, climbing and swimming and participated fully at school. Of course, life had its ups and downs which were managed along the way, but our lives followed a similar path to that of our family and friends. It wasn't until Jessica was nine years old that things started to change.

This book is written from a Mum's perspective, and it describes the journey we went through between 2010 and 2016, following the story of a slow onset of ME/CFS through various stages to full recovery. We are incredibly grateful to be able to share a story with a positive end, as so many in a similar situation are locked into this crippling condition for their whole life or for some severely affected may lose their lives. I hope that this story helps you to understand the everyday challenges we faced and plays a small part in helping to remove the stigma associated with this condition. Since its original label of 'yuppie flu' in the 1980's it seems astounding that more than forty years later there is still such a mass of anger, misconception and lack of understanding about the condition.

If you are caring for a loved one with ME/CFS or have the condition yourself, I hope this offers you some comfort to know that you are not the only one who has had to cope with the battles ahead and you can hope for a return to full health. Maybe our experience will help you to avoid some of the pitfalls we succumbed to. I wish you strength to know you can get through this, as we did.

If you are observing from a distance either as a friend, family member, perhaps an educator or health professional, I hope that you may eventually play a small part in changing perceptions, modifying treatment protocols and raising awareness as a result of our story, so that individuals and families can begin to receive the support they need and we can see an end to the unnecessary conflict, heartache, lack of understanding and suffering caused by this debilitating condition.

Before ME/CFS

At age nine, Jessica was attending a wonderful Junior School with caring and talented teachers and a head teacher who had great empathy and kindness. She was doing well at school and was a natural academic but also worked diligently to do her best. She had a group of lovely friends and enjoyed life.

One evening during the summer of 2006 Jessica went to bed as usual but came back downstairs ten minutes later crying and saying that she had hurt her neck. She felt really dizzy, had a bad headache and her vision was affected. If she looked at a page of writing the words spun upside down. She was very upset, and it was difficult to understand how she had managed to hurt her neck quite so badly just turning over in bed. I gave her an ice pack for her neck and some painkillers and eventually she settled down and went to sleep.

The next morning her neck was very stiff, and she had a constant headache that didn't appear to be eased with pain killers. We continued to apply ice regularly, but she was very uncomfortable and unable to go to school. We had hoped that after 24/48 hours she would be fine but that didn't turn out to be the case and her shoulder began to hurt as well. As she wasn't improving, I took her to a local chiropractor who advised that the headache was referred from her neck and that after four treatments she should be fully recovered as children tend to bounce back very quickly after such incidents. Jessica's injury appeared to be stubborn however and despite the chiropractic care and regular ice and rest there was no improvement.

We eventually sought the advice of a paediatric specialist who listened to our explanation of what had happened and ordered a CT scan. He asked her to rate her headache on a scale of 1-10 with 1 being very minor and 10 being the worst pain imaginable.

At this stage she said her headache scored around a 7-8 most of the time and we all got into the habit of asking for a daily pain score, just as the professionals were doing, ever hopeful that she would report a lower score and show some signs of improvement.

School suddenly became more challenging. Jessica found it difficult to sit at her desk and look at the whiteboard for long periods of time. I visited the school on numerous occasions to ask for their help and the teachers did what they could to sit her somewhere more suitable to avoid putting a strain on her neck. Almost daily there was an issue at school - she was finding her environment very challenging and reported that strong lights or heat made her headache worse. At any time when we hoped she was beginning to show signs of improvement it seemed that another event would knock her back. One day she was sitting with friends in the playground at lunch break with a group of boys playing football in the middle of the field. The ball came flying across the playground and hit Jessica on the head sending her neck into spasm and flaring up the headache and shoulder pain.

The results of the CT scan were fortunately clear, and the consultant decided she should try a course of migraine medication in case this was the route of the problem. We were grateful for the thorough investigation into every eventuality and did our utmost to downplay the situation to Jessica in order not to worry her. I was in regular contact with the school to seek their help but despite our efforts she was becoming anxious and felt unable to cope. We got through each day with another new idea to resolve the stream of issues coming our way, but the injury seemed highly irritable and the slightest wrong move could lock her shoulder up and exacerbate the head and neck pain. I clearly remember one day where our start to the morning had gone unusually well (up and dressed, breakfast eaten, bag packed and a timely exit from the house). I had driven Jessica to school and just as she was getting out of the car, she turned her head to look over her shoulder to wave to a friend and her neck went back into spasm. We sat in the car for a while, as she cried and I tried to comfort her, then I turned the car around to head for home and we got the ice pack out once more.

The migraine medication had no effect, so Jessica was referred for physiotherapy. We were prescribed some general neck mobility exercises and sent home to practice. Jessica was feeling demoralised by this point, but we did the exercises together and she diligently, albeit reluctantly, did them daily as instructed. Sadly, this also made no difference, and we were beginning to feel concerned at the amount of time it was taking to resolve the issue. Jessica's anxiety levels continued to increase, and, on many occasions, she had to contact the school receptionist to call me so that she could be taken home as her neck and head were so uncomfortable.

The school receptionist lacked empathy and Jessica always felt as though she was not believed. Although I had informed staff of the situation you could tell that the receptionist wasn't convinced and gave the impression that, as parents, we were being fooled by a child who just didn't want to be at school and was making excuses. What Jessica needed was some kindness and support, but all she received was an impatient response which grew with every incident that passed. Jessica knew she was unsympathetic and as a sensitive and polite child, was bemused by her treatment at the hands of an adult who was in a position of influence.

We sought second opinions from other health professionals and finally received treatment from another local, recommended chiropractor in the area. Initially there seemed to be some improvement and we were all delighted to being making progress. Despite months of treatment however the issue persisted, and I finally sought the advice of a physio acquaintance of mine. She listened carefully to the history of the issue and was thorough in her assessment, explaining the root cause of the problem in her opinion. She advised Jessica to do one specific neck strengthening exercise twice a day and finally this completely resolved the pain and instability in Jessica's neck. I very much wished I had sought her advice from the outset because the issue had dragged on for a long time and it had taken a toll on Jessica's confidence.

In September of 2012, Jessica started Secondary School. She was still in the midst of the neck and headache issues at the time, and I went to great lengths to contact the new school to inform them of the problem so that we could create a management plan for her well in advance. The school tried to find some ways to assist her but none of the solutions really helped. At one stage Jessica was offered a red card, which granted her an opportunity to present the card to any teacher in class and to be allowed, without question, to leave the room if her headache was getting really bad and her neck was sore and stiff. Although a useful idea, Jessica hated drawing attention to herself and was therefore reluctant to use the card. If she did use it, she was left alone to wander the school corridors and try to find a place of solitude for some respite, often berated by passing teachers for her time out of class and with many toilets locked, she had nowhere to go. Numerous visits, phone calls and emails made no difference to the reality of Jessica being swallowed up in a very large school with no way of supporting her.

The light and heat sensitivity increased, and the school environment became arduous. Some school rules were difficult to defend including a stipulation that blazers had to be kept on until an email had been sent to advise pupils that they were allowed to take them off. During hot weather Jessica would sit in her blazer, too afraid to ask if she could take it off for risk of looking silly in front of the rest of the class. She would overheat, her headache would worsen, and she would start to feel really unwell.

In addition to managing these issues, Jessica started being bullied. She has beautiful, long ginger hair but that led her to be the brunt of some very unkind behaviour. From hair pulling, to being tripped over, having her bags stolen during an assembly and kicked around the hall alongside relentless verbal 'ginger' assaults, her days in school were miserable. She didn't feel safe and with the ongoing headache and neck issues, she was vulnerable and fragile. Every day I would be waiting to hear from her hoping that a day could pass when she didn't feel open to attack. The school did not have control of bullying and school life for Jessica was torturous. We had further meetings with the school, Jessica was moved from one tutor group to another and we continued to believe that the school would take action and things would improve, as Jessica desperately wanted to stay at the same school as her friends. If it hadn't been for this plea we would have removed her from the school long before.

At this same time, my father was terminally ill. Having had prostate cancer diagnosed ten years earlier, the treatment had prolonged his life but sadly in February of 2012 we were told that the cancer had spread to his bones, and he only had nine months to live. My Dad had always been a large part of Jessica and her brother's lives and we had many happy holidays together where my Dad would sit quietly with his 'cherub' playing Sudoku puzzles and making up long division sums for her to practice. They all swam together in the sea and played cards and board games and every Sunday, my Mum and Dad would share a Sunday roast with us. We kept as much of the heartache away from the children as you inevitably would but on October 21st

2012, my Dad passed away. Jessica, her brother and both cousins were deeply upset and although they showed their emotions quite differently, it profoundly affected them all.

In November of that year, Jessica started to feel really unwell. She began to complain of a sore throat, swollen glands, continued headache, muscle aches and tiredness. The doctor told us it was a virus and Jessica was off school for a while but when a fortnight had passed and she was still feeling unwell, we felt pressurised to get her back to school in the hope that she would steadily get better.

During this time, her absence statistics were being continually highlighted to us and we regularly received official warning letters through the post advising that the school could take legal action against us if our child's attendance did not meet the desired levels. Attendance statistics were a huge focus and priority at the school - they offered award ceremonies for those with 100% attendance whilst penalising those who were absent including denying access to special movie afternoons, eliminating the possibility of gaining credits to become head boy/girl and threatening to deny access to the special events like the Year 11 Prom. Statistics were reported for entire tutor groups and Jessica felt to blame for her group's poor attendance figures. One event sticks in my mind where Jessica and a small group of other 'poor attenders' were denied access to an end of term movie - there were a few individuals who were disruptive and possible avoiders of the school environment but alongside our compliant daughter was a boy in a huge plaster cast as a result of breaking his leg severely and being in hospital for a prolonged period of time. They were all treated to the same punishment and Jessica spent the evening trying to make sense of why she and the boy with the broken leg were dealt with so harshly as they were both suffering enough already. We couldn't disagree and were feeling huge amounts of pressure to push her back in to school even though we knew she really wasn't well enough to cope. She would have a few days of feeling better and then a few days of feeling very unwell again. We were all confused and despite sincere attempts to do everything we could to get back to a routine, at every turn there seemed to be a new barrier that appeared. We kept hanging onto the hope that tomorrow would be different, and all this would soon be behind us.

We finally had to come to terms with the fact that 'something' really wasn't right, so we made a formal appointment with the Deputy Head teacher to discuss her absence figures. Until this point we had both counted on her making a full recovery and just getting back on with life as usual but our belief in this possibility had now been eroded away and we had to face facts. We were therefore grateful for the appointment and even though we couldn't explain what was happening, we needed to take stock of a situation which was worsening as time went by.

I prepared a huge amount of background information and took letters from consultants and GP appointment cards as evidence. We were initially made to feel as if we were making it all up, that we weren't supporting our daughter's attendance at school and that her absence was due to generalised anxiety.

Jessica certainly did have very high levels of anxiety at this time. She had started to have panic attacks on the way to school, her headaches were now more severe and she had a persistent sore throat and a tiredness that was not eased by sleep. She began being violently sick some mornings without warning which at first, we assumed was food poisoning and then perhaps an intolerance to something she was eating at breakfast. One morning she set off to walk to school with her friends having been sick and sitting for a while on the bottom of the stairs breathing slowly and deeply and trying all the relaxation techniques we had suggested. She managed to get out of the door and tried to chat happily with a smile on her face, so her friends didn't know anything was wrong. Jessica always put on a brave face and diligently did everything we suggested to her, trying desperately get back in control of her body. She only made it five minutes along the road before her best friend called to say she was having a panic attack. Her loyal and loving friend walked her home and I spent much of the rest of that morning trying to calm her down and reassure her. She felt publicly humiliated in the middle of the school rush on a path that was full of hundreds of children making their way to class. Everyone looked and stared at her. She couldn't keep up a front anymore and of course the longer this went on the more classes she missed and the more behind she became with her schoolwork.

The panic attacks weren't just related to the school environment. One evening we had arranged to go to the cinema with her best friend and Mum to see a film we had all been longing to see. We were excited to go and at the time Jessica seemed well. We arrived at the cinema and went to a screen room which was small and almost empty. We had deliberately chosen seats at the rear to ensure Jessica had as much space and fresh air around her as possible and everything seemed fine until halfway through the film when Jessica started to have a panic attack. We all did everything we could to help and eventually she became calmer, but we left to head for home at that point as she was in no state to stay and watch the film to the end.

Jessica is a conscientious and clever girl and was devastated to see her peers progressing ahead academically as she fell further behind, and the school did not provide a platform to catch up on topics she had missed. When she was in school, she was presented with a test on a subject she had never studied; when she was at home, she would be sent a worksheet on a topic she had never been taught. I bought every revision guide available and tried to help Jessica as much as I could creating copious revision notes for her so that she could learn subjects she was never taught for exams that were coming up. It was an uphill struggle and despite my greatest efforts nothing worked. Jessica's best friend also tried immensely hard to help as much as she could. Her best friend would call by every evening on her way home from school having tried to obtain extra notes or information from teachers. We would photocopy the notes and try to make some sense of it as we chatted together. She tried to explain concepts to Jessica and her friend's Mum and I spent every day texting or speaking to try to engineer a workable solution and make a plan to fill the huge voids in Jessica's learning that was growing day by day. Jessica's twelve-year-old best friend demonstrated more kindness, empathy and practical support than any member of school staff.

The school had labelled Jessica as a school 'refuser'. I remember quite vividly being told that Jessica had been watched one day in the playground and that she had been 'playing and running around with other children very happily'. They inferred that she was making it all up and pulling the wool over our eyes. Every interface with the school felt like I was going in to battle and I became used to defending our daughter from assumptions people made when seeing her for a short period of time.

The meeting with the Deputy Head teacher went on for a very long time. She was generous in the time she gave us and as time went on, she began to understand what a sad and difficult situation we were in.The mood in the room changed from one of doubt, cynicism and questioning, to one of genuine support, respect and concern over the events that were being explained. She thanked us at the end of the meeting for our gracious, affable manner and said how she appreciated the time it had taken to articulate the events in an understandable and logical manner so that she could help us. Without any medical explanation available, and yet presented with the reality of our daughter's ongoing poor attendance at school, action had to be taken. It was then that we were introduced to the Inclusion Unit (IU).

Viral Infection

The sore throats, headaches and tiredness went on and on. Just when we thought Jessica was bouncing back and had resumed everyday activities, she would become ill again.

One warm, sunny day Jessica and her best friend had been roller skating at the local common. They had been out for hours and had thoroughly enjoyed themselves. We were so happy that she was feeling well and enjoying herself. That evening she curled up under a blanket on the sofa with a sore throat, headache and aching joints. We assumed she had come down with a bout of flu and she spent days on the sofa with flu-like symptoms but never had a temperature which seemed unusual. Her nights became very disturbed. Most nights she would be unable to get to sleep as her headache was so bad. Medication had no effect and the later she dropped to sleep the more reluctant we were to wake her in the mornings. At its worst, she was awake until 5 am and only then dropped off to sleep. I felt that there was no way I could wake her after only two hours sleep, as she was already so exhausted, so we left her to sleep through the morning. We were sure that with a week of rest and care at home she would soon be back on the mend as the flu virus got out of her system.

This wasn't to be the case however and a pattern started to emerge. She would regularly have bouts of flu-like symptoms and after any period of feeling unwell, we were all so overjoyed that she was feeling better, we encouraged her to dive back into life and get straight back to everything she had been missing. Jessica remained optimistic and was always delighted to be back doing everything her friends were doing never questioning the regularity with which this strange flu seemed to reappear. We would always start each day with positivity and assume that life

was back to normal only to find that a few days later the flu would return. Over time
her symptoms became more widespread including insomnia, poor temperature regulation, the same constant headache, muscle and joint pain (particularly in her legs and knees), a continued sensitivity to bright light, noise and heat, problems concentrating, dizziness, heart palpitations, tiredness (that sleep never refreshed), stomach pains and vomiting. We were at a loss to know what was going on. Each and every day we would hope that the day had finally arrived when she would be able to stay well but her health continued to decline.

Despite numerous conversations with our GP, many appointments and several blood tests, we had no answers so I began to search the internet in desperate need of any clues as to what might be going on. I couldn't believe there wasn't an explanation and that no one else had ever gone through the same or a similar experience to us. I spent all my spare time trawling through information and finally read about the symptoms of ME/CFS. It seemed a possibility so I booked an appointment to discuss it with our GP in the hope that a confirmed diagnosis would get Jessica well again and we would finally be able to explain to the school, family and friends what we were dealing with.

Armed with this newfound knowledge, I went back to the GP and shared my suspected diagnosis. The GP agreed that it was most likely Jessica had ME/CFS and I was surprised this had never been suggested before. I had the distinct impression that it was a diagnosis that meant very little … it gave the symptoms a name, but the medical profession didn't really know what to do with it. We came away with a referral to a pediatrician at our local hospital and had to wait for an appointment to come through the post. All the while and with every delay, Jessica was becoming increasingly and more frequently unwell.

During this time, school was progressively more difficult. Jessica was unable to participate in mainstream education and had been placed on a reduced timetable, managed and implemented through the Inclusion Unit located at the back of the school, whose role it was to try to support those with special needs.

Our first encounter with the Inclusion Unit was one of mixed feelings. We knew that sadly Jessica could not now cope with mainstream schooling and were grateful for help. For us, it was a slightly intimidating place – one, relatively small building with two large rooms. The first was at the front of the building, with sofas and a small kitchenette and toilets. The second was a room at the back, overlooking a garden. The rooms were adjoined by a very small, internal space - full of PC's and several teachers, working on a one-to-one basis with other pupils. The front room was for anxious, school phobic, unwell or injured children and the rear room was for non-compliant children some of whom had exhibited bullying behaviour. Detentions were held in the back room.

An experienced teacher managed the IU and took her three large dogs to work every day to help the children. The dogs were a real advantage. Without them I don't feel Jessica would have ever had the courage to stay in the IU. Jessica found this teacher intimidating and the environment very frightening; to know that just next door she could be faced with one of the children who had bullied her was disturbing. The environment certainly did nothing to help matters but we were positive that reducing her timetable and having a more manageable day would bring forth benefits. The teacher showed some empathy and explained that her role had to be divided in order to manage both rooms - she used the analogy of having to wear two hats. The hats became inevitably muddled as she was naturally firm even when trying to be compassionate. There were occasions of real thoughtfulness from this teacher however, like the day she arranged for Jessica to go out of the school to walk the dogs, and another to go fruit picking, and the couple of times when she went to the local swimming pool with another girl in the IU. These opportunities took the pressure off the academic set back momentarily.

The IU staff worked with us to agree a reduced timetable. Jessica was removed from her existing tutor group and placed into the IU tutor group. She started her day later so that she was able to sleep in following the sleepless nights, and some non-essential subjects were removed from her curriculum. Looking back, this was all rather too little too late, but we had no idea what we were dealing with at the time and any support was welcomed by us. For Jessica however it was all a downward spiral. To be removed from mainstream education, to be 'different' and isolated, and yet with no known reason why she was feeling so ill most of the time was very disheartening. Many a lunch break was spent trying to find her friends within the school grounds. Often, they would be involved with clubs or special pursuits in which Jessica was unable to join in. She was offered the option to eat her lunch in a spare classroom to avoid the noise, bright lights and looks and stares she took to heart and her best friend always did her best to be with Jessica whenever she could. It was an uphill struggle and most days I would collect our exhausted daughter, who had achieved no benefit from her day and just suffered from trudging through the sheer torment that each hour presented to her. She learned nothing and wasted so much energy in doing so.

The focus of the school was of course still on academic achievement. Jessica had been predicted A or A* grades, performing very well across all subjects and had a prospective glorious school career ahead of her with academic success available if she kept the pressure up with her studies. We would receive regular reports on her grade achievements and once in the IU this pressure did not dwindle. We were regularly reminded that if she wanted to get A's or A*'s we must keep up the academic pressure. The process for passing work from the subject teacher to the IU was haphazard at best. Work was often not provided, not marked, not appropriate or as so often occurred was yet another test on a subject that Jessica had never been taught. It was demoralising to be told to sit a test when you clearly have no possible way of answering the questions only then to be told that your grade was poor, and you were falling behind. I tried endlessly to email teachers to try to get work sent home or given to the IU and to implore them not to give her another test, but nothing ever worked. Her best friend reported that Jessica's name was still on the old tutor group register, and that every morning her name was called and every day she was marked absent, a harsh and very public affirmation of her absenteeism. Other children would ask her best friend questions about her whereabouts and why Jessica wasn't attending mainstream classes, but there were no answers. We all just continued to have ever increasing questions.

Jessica continued to learn nothing. Her health continued to decline and the rationale to step foot inside the school each day seemed wholly focused on facing her anxiety and not succumbing totally to her presumed school phobia.

We eventually received the pediatric appointment, and all our hopes were pinned on the meeting with a specialist at the local General Hospital. We were greeted by a doctor, who listened for a brief while about the decline in Jessica's health and our suspected diagnosis. He concurred with the GP that although there was no test to formally diagnose ME/CFS, he was also certain this was what she was experiencing. At that point, amongst other tests, he decided to do some additional blood tests. One of these was a test to see if Jessica had ever had Glandular Fever - a test we had never been offered before. The results were conclusive. She had most certainly had Glandular Fever in the past as antibodies were present in her blood and he believed that this was the most probable cause of the onset of her prolonged illness. Apparently, this is a common initiator for post viral fatigue and then chronic fatigue/ME as symptoms are often missed and as in our case, the collection of symptoms is just put down to a generalised virus. Rushing recovery is not helpful and looking back that is exactly what we felt obliged to do.

Around the same time as the onset of Jessica feeling really unwell, her best friend had been diagnosed with Glandular Fever. She had felt poorly for a while and been off school and at home trying to rest and get herself better. She was unable to eat due to nausea, became very weak and was eventually taken to hospital by ambulance. After flooding her body with fluids and minerals and taking blood tests to reveal the Glandular Fever, she began to improve. It took some long time however to get fully well and I remember her Mum recounting the tale of a day at school when her daughter nearly collapsed. As a result, she had sat on the curb side with her for some long time until she was able to get her into the car and home. Glandular Fever is caused by the Epstein-Barr Virus. Symptoms include sore throat, swollen glands, tiredness and a temperature. It is a highly contagious condition and easily passed from one person to another. Most people recover in two to four weeks, but the tiredness can last for months. We were amazed this had been missed but at the time the complexity of Jessica's symptoms probably clouded any such diagnosis. It was clear now that Jessica and her best friend must have picked up Glandular Fever at the same time. Jessica's best friend's Mum and I remarked at how curious it was that neither of us had really considered this at the time. Looking back, it all now seemed so obvious but during that period it was anything but.

We were sent home from the Pediatricians office with a one page, A4, photocopied sheet of paper on how to deal with ME/CFS. It was woefully inadequate in terms of advice but offered a few suggestions; a one liner about not doing too much and amongst other random and sparse suggestions recommended reviewing sleep hygiene protocols in order to re-establish a restful night's sleep. We arrived home with various feelings; relief that we finally had confirmation of a diagnosis from a specialist, satisfaction that we knew the root cause of her illness and disbelief that we only had one sheet of paper with poor advice on how to get her better. We set to work reviewing Jessica's sleep hygiene as recommended on the pediatrician's sheet. She already had no TV in her room, no phone or other electronic gadgets, her room was well ventilated, cool, quiet and dark and she was listening to calming music/sounds and using relaxation apps. She had a new mattress, a tidy bedroom and loved to read at bedtime. There didn't seem to be any more we could do. Her erratic temperature fluctuations and poor sleep pattern continued but at least I knew we had considered everything that was suggested.

The one other thing we came away from the Pediatricians office with was a referral to CAMHS (Child and Adult Mental Health Services). CAMHS were already overwhelmed and with too few staff the waiting lists were long. It took many months for an appointment to come through at the General Hospital but eventually we received a booking with a lovely counsellor. She was friendly, kind and compassionate and listened patiently to the long story of Jessica's declining health. At the end of the discussion, she understood how Jessica had become so anxious as a result of the health issues she had been dealing with and the worry of trying to make sense of such a poorly understood condition. She wrote copious notes for the Pediatrician but aside from that was unable to offer any practical support as by this time any exertion made Jessica feel much worse. This included travelling to and from places, meeting with friends or extended family or anything that used up physical, emotional or cognitive energy. It was pleasant however to speak with someone who understood the challenges we were facing as nearly everyone else we met couldn't grasp the issues. She would have happily arranged weekly counselling sessions but could see very clearly that the journey and appointment time would have made Jessica ill for several days afterwards. We all agreed that nothing was to be gained from her intervention and so we left after a draining session without any tangible, positive outcome except for yet another relaxation tape and a photocopied A4 sheet on breathing. Breathing exercises, mindfulness, meditation, relaxation apps, self-help books, Yoga, Pilates... Jessica had tried it all. I had read many books on managing anxiety and panic disorders and she had tried every breathing technique suggested. All of these interventions seemed completely insufficient as the illness took hold.

At the follow up appointment with the Pediatrician he suggested she start taking Beta-blockers to help to manage the condition and prescribed Propranolol. The mass of symptoms and anxiety just kept getting worse and after a few months with no improvement we were not prepared to continue with the medication.

We went armed to the school with the diagnosis, hoping that this information would make a difference. We had waited for almost two years to have a diagnosis and it felt like a huge step forward. The reality however was that it made no difference at all - no-one knew what to do with it and nothing changed. Jessica slowly and steadily went downhill.

We continued to reduce Jessica's timetable and limit the time that she was in school. She still went into the IU when she was well enough but with her health being so variable from day to day and hour to hour her attendance continued to drop. There are many unhappy memories around this time, but one stands out above all others.

At the end of Year 8, Jessica's friends were attending a lunchtime drama club and as she so longed to do something with her friends and particularly enjoyed acting, we supported her enthusiasm to attend. She liked the club very much and it gave her a glimmer of enjoyment but without any major commitment, as she was too unwell to manage anything longer term. She had already had to stop all of her out of school activities, dropping out of two theatre groups that she had belonged to for several years. One day, the drama teacher announced that everyone had to stay after lunch and work into the first lesson of the next period to rehearse a mini production that was to be presented to a small group of other students. All teachers were supposed to be aware of Jessica's situation and reduced timetable but to make sure, Jessica politely reminded her that she had to go home straight after lunch. The teacher reacted by telling everyone in the club that Jessica was letting them all down as she wasn't prepared to stay and that if the piece didn't come together properly it was all her fault. Such a public shaming absolutely crucified an already fragile Jessica who appeared at the car, where I was waiting to take her home, in floods of tears. It wasn't until sometime after we arrived home that she was able to calm down enough to formulate her words and explain what had happened. Shortly afterwards I received a call from her best friends Mum to say that she had been called to collect her daughter from school as she was inconsolable at the appalling treatment her best friend had received from this teacher. Her best friend knew more than anyone else what this meant to

Jessica and how in one moment the teacher had dealt a hugely damaging blow to her. Several of her friends were in tears after that event. They all knew of her illness, the reduced timetable and how much the club meant to Jessica. She had to give up the club and it was another loss in what was by now a growing list of disappointments. As this was at the end of term, we consoled ourselves with the thought that we had six weeks over the Summer to rebuild her strength and confidence, get her well and prepare her for a new term. Despite our efforts however she only managed one day of Year 9 and spent the rest of the year housebound and extremely unwell.

Acting, singing and dancing had always been a highlight for Jessica and since the age of seven she had enjoyed attending local Stagecoach classes. Every Saturday, Jessica and her best friend would spend three hours during the afternoon, enjoying a range of performing arts activities and once a year this would culminate in a Summer show. There were also special Charity Shows and summer workshops to attend, all of which Jessica was keen to do. Several annual highlights had been booked over the years whilst Jessica was deteriorating in health and all required significant logistical arrangements to ensure she could participate. With our newly acquired diagnosis, but no real advice regarding management, we were always conscious of her limited energy supplies and the multitude of symptoms that would appear when her body was pushed too far. We therefore tried everything we could to ease the energy burden for events to make sure that she could still join in with shows and take part alongside her friends. There was a performance on a London stage at the Shaftesbury Theatre that she had been looking forward to very much so I drove her and her friend to London, whilst the rest of the ensemble went by coach. Fortunately, I managed to park relatively close to the Theatre, packed drinks and plenty of food and made a bed in the open boot of the car where Jessica could lie out and rest between the Technical, Dress Rehearsals and the actual performance. It was a very long day and a huge challenge for her but she was determined to get through to the evening show. Her barrage of symptoms were in full swing; she almost fainted twice; once in a shop nearby where her best friend and I sat on the floor with her whist she recovered enough to get back to the car and another time when trying to walk up the stairs backstage to the dressing rooms. She sat on the stairs, head in hands, deep breathing until she felt a little better and was able to get up the final few stairs to where she needed to be. The Stagecoach girls were wonderful, as was the principal and his wife. They were all incredibly supportive and caring of her and couldn't do enough to try to help wherever possible. I appreciated this very much and so did Jessica. She always referred to them as her Stagecoach family and they held a very special place in her life. It was very sad when her illness progressed to a point where she could no longer attend the weekly three hour sessions and despite whittling it down to two hours and then just one, it finally became too much and she had to stop. Even then however, the organisation were sensitive to her plight and offered a scholarship for continued attendance as and when she was well enough to rejoin. This was a very welcome gesture and finally allowed her to proudly accept her ten year award in 2018. These are the type of people that we wished we had been surrounded by more.

Regrettably, episodes like that of the Year 8 Drama teacher were all too common. On one other occasion, Jessica had spent days building herself up to get into school after a bout of flu-like symptoms. This long wait to feel well made us all desperate for her day of attendance to be a positive and fulfilling one. I dropped her at the IU as usual for her short stay and waited at home hoping to hear good news. It turned out that this particular day had been designated for a fire drill. The usual regime is for all students to assemble on the school field within their tutor groups in alphabetical order. At that time no one had explained to Jessica that she had been registered to the IU tutor group, she had no idea of the other students in the group so was unable to recognise anyone and as her name was reportedly still being called on her old tutor group register, she assumed she should line up with them. Confused and faced with the prospect of walking across and around the field to find her old tutor group and friends (bearing in mind that all physical exertion was using up her limited energy supplies) she eventually found where she thought she should be and had to line up in between the boys who had bullied her in Year 7. The boys who had stolen her bag, pulled her hair, drawn pictures of her as a witch and called her ugly were now surrounding her. The boys began a barrage of questions and comments; "Where have you been ? What's wrong with you? Are you in IU?" and then amused themselves by shouting at each other to get away from her as she was contagious and backed away from her laughing.

Most days at school filled Jessica with disappointment at not being able to join in with her friends. She was already feeling defeated and we were keen that she had some positive moments to keep her going. At the end of Year 8 the school were holding auditions for their next show, 'The Sound of Music' and Jessica rallied the energy and hopes to audition alongside her friends. I remember clearly receiving an email from the head of the drama department telling me that Jessica had been successful in securing a main part as one of the Von Trapp children. I was so proud of her, she had sung beautifully and received great praise for her audition, which was gladly received and much needed at that point, but we all knew deep down that she would never be able to cope with the punishing rehearsal schedule that arrived with the offer of the part. Jessica's heart sank as she read the schedule and the momentary feeling of elation passed and she returned to her standard state – that of resigned disappointment.

During Year 8, another student arrived in the IU with ME/CFS and attended for one hour a day. The girl was older than Jessica and in her final year of GCSE's. We were told that she was receiving specialist help from a team at Bath hospital. The school kindly contacted the girls mum and asked if she could give me her telephone number. The girl's Mum was happy to help and gave me as much information as she could about the Bath team and how to get a referral to that department via the NHS. I felt renewed optimism that this would be a route to positive change as I contacted the Bath team and made an appointment.

Grasping at Straws

The exact timing of the course of events over the four years of Jessicas illness is slightly blurry. There were long spells whilst we waited for specialist appointments and many times spent looking for ways to make Jessica better. Life had been put on hold to a certain degree whilst I was fully preoccupied with finding ways we could get Jessica out of this downward spiral of ill health.

I was lucky enough to have a part time job, which offered me a little time to escape the otherwise endless thoughts and investigations in to how we were going to get our little girl better. Teaching and practicing Pilates was a true blessing. In every way it helped me to get through those agonising years with a positive and determined outlook. I would share a personal, private lesson with my very good friend and colleague once a fortnight and she always listened to the events of the previous two weeks and offered much valued, logical suggestions along the way. This short mental and physical break away from our all absorbing situation certainly provided me with a well needed change and the restorative and refreshing effects were most welcome. We learnt that our teacher (and by then friend and colleague) had also suffered with ME/CFS for eight years and she kindly shared the story of her experience. It was heartening to see her moving with such control, grace and strength and she gave me a regular boost of optimism - to become a movement teacher, having escaped the years of confinement and inactivity was a tangible, physical display of what could be possible and I hoped we may experience the same for Jessica one day. During these times, if Jessica was at home, my Mum would often come and sit with her. As the ME/CFS progressed, Jessica was too weak to be left alone most of the time and I was so fortunate to have my Mum just around the corner and ever willing to play her part in supporting us.

As soon as we received the diagnosis we embarked on a long and varied journey to try different healing solutions and ensure that we left no stone unturned in our efforts to return to life as we had once known it. With professional medical advice seriously lacking, we accepted that we needed to find our own way through this situation and we weren't prepared to dismiss any possibility that may offer a cure, even those that seemed unlikely or improbable. I must admit to moments of feeling totally helpless but with every new plan came new hope and we wanted to keep a totally open mind to all possibilities.

Jessica started to have regular counselling sessions with a local, well respected and experienced Gestalt therapist. Her anxiety had developed to a fairly high level by this time and she was having regular panic attacks. She would now often be violently sick in the mornings and was still not sleeping at night. Jessica went to see the counsellor for several months and patiently attended the sessions even though she did not enjoy them or feel any benefit. She did not respond well to the techniques and reacted very poorly to tapping sequences the counsellor showed her. The technique called EFT (Emotional Freedom Technique) involves a series of tapping patterns on the body to stimulate meridian points thereby reducing stress and negative emotions and restoring balance to disrupted energy systems. Jessica did not want to be touched or tapped, she was highly cynical of the concept and was often too depressed to even try.

Undeterred, we sought the help of a private, specialist clinic in London founded by Alex Howard the author of 'Why Me?', a book written about his experiences of ME and route back to health. I read his book among many others as my preoccupation with finding out as much as I could about this unknown condition went on and on.

I had by this time read and heard from many sources that dietary issues were often linked to the condition and despite always taking care of our family's nutrition we decided to seek detailed input in the event that some clue could be derived from the findings. If there was some kind of food that was producing inflammation within Jessica, or if she had a nutrient deficiency that needed supplementation, we were desperate to find out - anything to understand what was keeping her is a perpetual state of illness. The clinic initiated a series of tests including adrenal stress tests, leaky gut syndrome investigations and allergy tests to determine whether Jessica was showing signs of specific issues or lacking in any essential vitamins and minerals that might support her back to good health. We did a multitude of tests via the post and GP, all of which offered no insights. We tried magnesium salts for baths, magnesium supplements, magnesium body rubs plus a vast array of different vitamins, minerals and specialist foods. Jessica's appetite however had now started to be affected and she was eating less and less. She always had a peculiar 'hot' throat and spent hours sucking ice lollies to try to alleviate the feeling. By now, she was certainly not receiving a well-balanced set of nutrients from her food as she ate the same thing each day, so the supplements provided some small reassurance that we were doing our best for her body under the circumstances. We completed every test the clinic offered and all tests came back normal. The only test we didn't do was a Mitochondrial function test which was not a test supported by the NHS and would have required lengthy and difficult arrangements to complete. I would have been more than prepared to do anything that led us down a path to a cure but it was evident to us that we had reached a point where further tests were most likely going to be more damaging to Jessica than they were helpful. She had already had so many tests in her life and seen so many different experts all without success that it became clear her morale was sinking and she was losing all hope. The psychological impact of this condition was hitting her with full force and we needed to change direction.

At one stage, having reached the point of complete desperation, we sought the services of a spiritual healer. A friend had told me of his healing powers and the effect he had on her mother-in-law after a diagnosis of cancer. The healer had appeared in newspapers and magazines and had a long waiting list of new clients. His treatment room was at the back of his house approximately 45 minute's drive away. Jessica was extremely disbelieving but to her great credit, as always, she reluctantly went along with my positive, upbeat determination for this new plan. I wanted to believe that this could be a cure. Anything was worth a try at this stage, after all, the condition had baffled current medical science so we may swell explore other avenues. My Mum came along for the ride, ever supportive and also eager to believe in a new approach.

We arrived to a full waiting room with newspaper cuttings posted all over the walls of amazing cures the healer had performed. An old TV played a video on a constant loop with his clients explaining the miracles he had performed upon them. One cutting on the wall was the story of the cure of a young lady with ME/CFS. I read that article with such joy and hoped that we too could soon be enjoying our lives again. The small treatment room was very warm with a log burning fire constantly working even in the heat of summer. A full-sized statue of a Red Indian stood in the corner of the room with a white dove sitting on top. The whole statue was covered in bird droppings and as we were ushered in to the room by the healer we were handed a wet wipe each to clean off the chairs before sitting on them! My Mum is petrified of birds and yet she still accepted the wet wipe and obediently cleaned her chair before sitting down. She endured the experience remarkably well, closing her eyes and holding her breath whenever the bird came anywhere near to her and we both took every moment of it very seriously. The healer sat Jessica on a low stool in front of him and placed his hands in various places on her back, neck and shoulders. He asked her to close her eyes and enquired whether she saw any particular colours or felt any heat from his hands. Despite my hopes that one day she would see some symbolic colour and we would witness a healing miracle in front of our eyes, we never did. Nothing changed, well nothing positive anyway – the only difference was the clear toll the journey time was taking on her health. Even if she had perceived some minor improvement after the session, by the time we arrived home she was drained, exhausted and had a sickly, grey pallor which became a regular visible sign of her state of health.

On one occasion Mum was with Jessica as she was feeling really unwell and I was coming home from work to collect them both and drive to the appointment. Jessica had fallen down the stairs and her neck had gone into spasm. After the tears and drama had subsided and we knew she wasn't badly hurt, Mum and I debated long and hard whether to take her. We both agreed that we couldn't miss a potential opportunity for a miracle, and of course today could have been THE day so we drove to the healer. She couldn't move her neck and sat rigidly in the car all the way there, unable to look left or right. I told the healer of the accident and he lay his hands on her as usual, repeating the quiet ritual we now recognised. As we drove away, she wasn't cured but her neck pain was significantly better which at least seemed to justify the journey there and back.

Specialist Help

Jessica's best friend's Mum, my neighbour and good friend, was an amazing support for me from the outset and I benefited greatly from her thoughts, wisdom and kindness. Amongst the concern and kindness offered by family and other friends, her proximity and the girls shared relationship ever since they were both just one year of age, made her my greatest support. During the very difficult times when Jessica was housebound, she and I would walk to the local Junior School on a Friday afternoon whenever we could to collect our sons. She always made time for an extended walk so that I could get some fresh air and download the emotions of the week. The escape from our four walls was much needed and valued.

She had the amazing capacity for perfect timing, impeccable intuition and a deep empathy. We first met when we moved into our new home in May 2002. My husband had been out and about with Jessica and bumped into her when returning from the local park. I vividly remember him walking in the front door whilst I was unpacking boxes and telling me excitedly that he had met another Mum and little girl with whom we could make friends.

Watching your daughter deteriorate in front of your eyes is heartbreaking and it has a profound effect on you. Looking back, I distinctly recall the feelings every morning whilst looking out of our kitchen window to the street outside. We live a short walk from the secondary school and on a popular shortcut that runs past our house. Each and every morning I watched streams of children getting themselves to school. I saw all of Jessica's friends walking past morning and evening and so wished that she was with them. It was harrowing to think so deeply about everything she was missing out on and in order to keep my spirits up and my resolve in good shape, I had to avoid looking out of the window at those times of the day; there was no point in torturing myself.

As time went on, friends lost interest in Jessica as she was absent from school more and more. They would still walk past our front door and I willed them to just drop a short note through the door or send a quick text to Jessica just to say hello. Jessica began to feel overwhelmingly lonely.

Her best friend however was a constant support, alongside that of one other very close friend. The girls were amazing in so many ways and I am truly grateful that they kept in contact. I couldn't imagine how we would ever have recovered the situation without their persistent, kind and unquestioning loyalty. Her best friend even struggled through thirty degree heat and a panic attack to run a 5km race with her Dad to raise money for an ME charity and support Jessica.

Aside from my friend and neighbour, one other Mum tried her very hardest to keep her daughter in contact with Jessica for as long as possible. Someone with whom we hadn't actually known for that long and yet was so thoughtful in her actions. She would regularly ask Jessica to bake her a cake, which gave a purpose to a day and was a manageable activity. I was very fortunate to have this additional support for although it was only on an infrequent basis, the timing was just right and when I was desperate for some small injection of someone else's help, she seemed to have an uncanny knack to get in contact.

I had moments like this relatively often. It is incredibly difficult to start each day, knowing you have to get right through to the end, with optimism, an undeterred spirit and with a constant supply of things to talk about, look at and do which isn't really doing anything at all. Those long hours stretching ahead seemed to go on forever and little things that would amuse Jessica and I were invaluable. Jessica's Grandma used to send cards in the post occasionally and these were very welcome. Hearing the postman at the door and being able to give Jessica something to open was a true highlight to an otherwise painful, long and arduous day. I recall watching Breakfast TV one day and hearing a report about a girl who was bed bound with ME/CFS who has started up a charity where small gifts were posted out to children who were too ill to go out. I would never have believed what a lovely feeling it is to receive something like that under normal circumstances but living with this condition opened my eyes to how important these small gestures are to get you through another day. Jessica and I would shop online for small gifts and I would wrap them to send to her charity. I hope the recipients enjoyed a brief spell of happiness from our parcels. We certainly benefited from doing it.

Having a child with ME/CFS is absolutely life changing for them, their parents, siblings and extended family but Jessica's brother was most definitely affected the most.

Jessica's younger brother was always very concerned for her. The two of them share a very special bond and seem closer than many siblings, sharing a similar temperament, enjoying many of the same things and seemingly, and effortlessly, 'in tune' with one another. Every day when he came home from school he would call out hello on the doorstep and await a response. On the days he was greeted with a reply from her he said he felt such relief as he knew she wasn't doing too badly that day, but on many an occasion he would receive no response at all and then he knew she was really suffering. He carried the worries over her health around with him every day. As time went on, and the ME/CFS got worse, he would watch his phone in fear of hearing that something really bad had happened to her. He thought she might die.

We finally received our appointment from the hospital in Bath. At this time Jessica was still in school for very limited periods but her health was deteriorating and although we were keen to go I was very concerned at the impact of such a long journey. I had researched the hospital website beforehand and was really impressed with the level of detail and information provided. It was very different to the to the single A4 sheet provided by the Paediatrician at our local hospital.

Esther Crawley was the lead professor in Child Health at the University of Bristol. She led the paediatric centre for young people at the RHNRD at Bath and we were to meet one of her team, a delightful young lady who was a physiotherapist. The journey exhausted Jessica and the consultation took a very long time, with many questions and detailed information provided about the management protocols we should now implement to start her on the path to recovery.

Esther had spent many years working with those afflicted with ME/CFS. I had watched her presenting a TED talk a short while before our appointment and was surprised to hear her say that she had received death threats, endured horrendous behaviour against her and admitted to working in an area surrounded by a great deal of controversy, At the time it seemed hard to understand why she would have had such an experience but as our knowledge of the illness grew we could see quite clearly the difficulties for those dealing with the illness personally or those trying to manage it.

She was a determined and dedicated professional who had created a management system to help those suffering with ME/CFS to cope with the condition and aid recovery. The system was based upon monitoring energy expenditure and the team at Bath had devised a colour coded chart that considered physical, mental and emotional exertion. It was sensitive to the fact that every individual is different and would therefore find some activities more draining than others. For the very first time I felt that we were talking to people who really understood the condition and it was a relief to have clear directions and a process to follow. I was happy that we no longer had to deal with this alone - that was a huge comfort and it made sense of the confusing array of symptoms and the up and down nature of the illness that had bewildered us for so long.

Every day we had a chart to fill in. The chart had each hour of every day of the week identified with a small box, which you marked in the colour of energy being used at that time. There were three levels of energy consumption: red, yellow and green. Red identified activities that used high levels of energy consumption. Depending on the severity of the ME/CFS this encompassed any physical exercise, attending school, social events, watching new TV, reading new books, any form of travel, talking on the telephone, being with friends, showering and eating meals at the table. Yellow highlighted moderate levels of energy expenditure and, depending on the severity of the ME/CFS, encompassed watching TV you have watched before, reading books you have read before, listening to audio books and talking quietly to parents/siblings. Green identified times of relaxation, meditation or complete rest but not sleep.

At the time of the appointment, we calculated that Jessica's tolerance for red activities was about three hours. This was referred to as her baseline. The principle was that you established a level of activity that could be achieved each day without having 'payback'. Payback is the term used to explain the flu-like symptoms that Jessica had been experiencing after exertion. The degree of payback i.e. the length and severity of symptoms were related to level of exertion, so the more you overdid it, the worse you felt and the longer you continued to feel unwell. The ups and downs of wellness and illness Jessica had been experiencing were called 'boom and bust'. All of these new ME/CFS terms were explained to us and I felt quite in awe of those who had devised a system to explain what we had been completely at a loss to understand.

The appointment dragged on and by the end Jessica was exhausted, her skin had turned the sickly pale grey colour we now recognised and she looked glazed as we left. Her brother had paid close attention to everything that was explained to us and completely understood what we all needed to do to get her well so we chatted on the way back about how we should implement the system at home. We would all do anything if it meant we could get Jessica well again.

The next challenge was to explain all of this to everyone else and that wasn't an easy task. The three of us had watched Jessica exhibit all of the now carefully explained ME/CFS symptoms over the years and for us it was a relief that we finally had words to label and express what we had witnessed for so long. It was reassuring to be in company where we had a shared language and to know we weren't alone in going through this horrible experience. The condition is experienced across all age groups, religions, races, genders and nationalities and yet many people have never heard of it and those who have do not understand it.

So it wasn't easy for those around us. The most difficult thing for most to accept was that Jessica could appear fine at a given time but the next day or even a few hours later would suffer terribly as the payback kicked in. No-one else saw the payback. All the outside world would see would be the days when she finally had a day of feeling well. The long days of pain, illness and isolation went unnoticed as she was locked up indoors. ME/CFS was explained to us like a faulty car battery. The body would drain itself of energy and, as a result, would suffer with a host of nasty symptoms and it would take several days of rest to recharge the battery. The aim of the Bath process was to find a baseline of activity that could be undertaken without fully draining this imaginary battery and then very slowly build up the tolerance to do more.

If someone has a broken bone, everyone understands and accepts the process to get better. We all realise that there is a period of immobility, rest and recuperation followed by a slow and gradual building back to normal activity. This was no different, aside from the fact that there was nothing to see and there were times when she appeared and looked well. No broken bone, no plaster cast and in fact no visible symptoms when she was in public (which was by now rarely). She could appear totally well one day and yet the next be very unwell. This is tricky to comprehend.

Those who saw us daily understood it the most. Those we saw less often struggled to understand. I doubt we would have truly believed it if we hadn't lived it.

Colour-Coded Living

Every day we would allocate three hours of red time, which we spread across the day in no more than thirty minute sections. This was something we found (through trial and error) worked for Jessica, as she certainly couldn't do all three hours in one go. We sectioned the day with as much yellow activity as we could think up and three, five minute green slots. One small red activity was always a walk outside to keep her mobility and strength up.

Jessica hated the green times of day. She described them as 'staring at the ceiling times' and became incredibly frustrated with them. She didn't find mindfulness possible and neither could she meditate. The breathing exercises were equally unhelpful as whenever she paid any attention to her breathing she felt dizzy and panicky as a result. She did try however as diligently as she always did everything she was asked to do including trying all types of breath patterns and in the end she just became cyclical of them. In fact Jessica found any focus on her body made all her symptoms seem worse so she preferred by far to find some form of distraction. We persevered with these suggested techniques for as long as we could and then accepted that they were counterproductive. Doing absolutely nothing for someone who is already locked in a body unable to do anything didn't seem logical and being depressed and alone with her thoughts would send her into a spiral.

Yellow time was initially based around watching repeat episodes of 'Friends' and this went on for a long time. I still can't watch an episode of that programme despite having loved it for many years. It was replayed over and over again whilst Jessica lay under a blanket on the sofa. She would re-read Harry Potter novels, which fortunately she still loves, and sit and chat to me. My daily mission became one of dreaming up new yellow activities. It was incredibly difficult to come up with something that is interesting enough to occupy and hour or so of time, that is still relaxing and non stimulating whilst offering variety to fill such a vast expanse of time.

We would try to dream up new and inventive ideas, just to break the tedium. Our collection of activities would include colouring, painting nails, looking at old photograph albums, tidying out cupboards (I did the tidying whilst Jessica observed and suggested what might need throwing away), me reading quiz books or facts books to her, flicking through a paper clothes catalogue or cookery book (any time on the computer was deemed red time). We played games that we used to play in the car on long journeys (like eye spy, the alphabet game, name your favourite... etc.) and even resorted to a game called 'making shapes from the pattern on the ceiling'. That was a particular favourite when she still couldn't get to sleep during the early hours of the morning and we would move bedrooms to stare at the artex on the spare room ceiling for a while and see if we could notice anything different to that her bedroom ceiling could offer. It was a full time job and I would be so pleased if I came up with a new idea. Anything to pass an hour of the day, try to amuse Jessica and keep her as happy as I could.

Night times were awful. Jessica would go to bed at the same time as we did. We would just be dropping off to sleep and she would open our door to say she couldn't sleep as her headache was so bad. During the day the constant headache was slightly more bearable. She tried hard to distract herself and it worked to a certain extent but when she was alone in the dark at night without any other focus, her head pain became overwhelming. We tried all types of painkillers, balms, hot and cold compresses on the back of her neck or on her forehead, supplements, foods high in magnesium, peppermint and lavender essential oils, acupuncture, herbal teas ... but nothing ever worked. Each time

I came up with a new idea to relieve the pain it gave us a few hours of hope. The GP gave her Co-codamol and various forms of migraine medication also to no avail. I would lie next to Jessica in her bed and massage her feet following directions online from Chinese Reflexology techniques. We would sit up and talk, play our ceiling pattern game and I would read to her. If swapping beds didn't work we would eventually go downstairs and put on yet another episode of Friends. We could be up until 3 am on a regular basis.

With all of these sleepless nights, we would leave Jessica asleep in the mornings until she woke naturally. The less sleep she had the worse she felt and so we did everything we could to try to maximise her rest. I would unplug the phone so it didn't wake her if anyone called in the mornings and we all crept around the house for fear of disturbing her. This seemed the right thing to do at the time. Her body clock went crazy. She would go to sleep at 4 or 5 am and wake up at 1pm.

This was one of the first changes the Bath team asked us to implement. We were to rigidly enforce strict wake up and bed times every day to get her body clock back on track. Every day she was to be woken at 8.30 am and bedtime was to be 10 pm. As she was so far away from this, we worked slowly to bring the times back to a regular pattern by waking her 30 minutes earlier every day. It was a tortuous fortnight and Jessica felt very ill for the whole time but by now we knew that it was the right course of action. If we didn't, Jessica was set to be up all night and asleep all day and I couldn't have functioned like that much longer. We ticked off the days until we made it to 8.30 am. It was a dreadful two weeks where Jessica experienced a lot of pain and felt extremely ill but it made a significant difference thank goodness.

Night times were also blighted with panic attacks. I am generally a light sleeper and have been ever since the children were born. We always slept with our door open but Jessica preferred hers closed. One night I woke to howling cry's and we both leapt out of bed and raced to Jessica's room to find her in the midst of a severe panic attack. She was absolutely rigid, crying and screaming and finding it hard to breathe. She said that she had been unable to move and couldn't get to our room for help. Neither of us heard her and we felt so awful that I went out and bought an alarm for her to have by her side in case it happened again. It took a long while to calm her down and fortunately her brother never stirred as far as we know. We were very grateful for that. The panic attacks were accompanied by severe stomach cramps which left her doubled over and we were never sure what each night would bring.

Such were the extent of her symptoms, that we became very confused about which were payback, and which were maybe something else. The stomach cramps were a perfect example. One night Jessica had to press her bedside alarm as she was doubled over in bed, in tears and rolling around in agony. She was having severe stabbing pains in her abdomen, which had been going on for some while. We tried hot water bottles, massaging, stretching, painkillers, cuddling and anything else I could come up with to try to ease the pains but nothing worked. After a couple of hours they started to subside. Within a few days she started her period and we assumed the pains must have been due to her menstrual cycle, which was very erratic. The trouble was these pains occurred at relatively frequent intervals and we had no idea whether they were a new form of payback or not.

She had frequent bouts of severe pain, either head pain, stomach pains or leg pains. The head pain was relentless and impossible to manage. Particularly during the evenings, her pain would worsen and we were helpless to offer any form of relief. Nothing worked and we had by that time tried absolutely everything. One particular evening we were at our wits end whilst she cried and thrashed around, banging her forehead with the pain. I felt my only course of action was to drive her to A&E. Our A&E department fortunately has a separate area for children and we were seen relatively quickly. After a series of further tests we were eventually sent home with the advice that it was just a symptom of the ME/CFS and there was nothing they could do to help. We drove home and thankfully Jessica dropped off to sleep at around 5am. To be told there is nothing the medical profession can do whilst you watch your child in significant pain is heartbreaking and one of the worst feelings a parent can experience I would imagine. It certainly was for me.

Chest pains were another symptom that developed much later and became worryingly severe. After such a long time of dealing with this condition I had almost become indifferent to all of these symptoms. It never became any easier watching her going through this awful torment but I suppose I had somehow casually put every symptom down to ME as that is what we had always been told. We had one episode however during a mid-morning where Jessica started to roll around on her bed holding her chest and crying. These chest pains were so significant and new (we had experienced most symptoms but never chest pains before) and nothing we tried seemed to help, so I dialled 111 to ask for advice. Having been through the questions asked by the responder on the telephone she decided that an ambulance must be called so we waited for the crew to arrive. By this time the pains were starting to abate thankfully and I felt like such a fraud when the blue lights appeared and a crew of three paramedics arrived. I was very apologetic for calling them out as the pains has now eased but they were so professional, caring and supportive. Jessica was petrified this whole time thinking that she must be in a very serious state for an ambulance to be needed and was sure she must therefore be having a heart attack. My blasé approach to yet another symptom at this stage seemed reckless and I was keen for their assessment of her. After plugging her in to their machines and watching her normal heart trace we were all reassured and the crew were jovial and good humoured throughout, providing us with every reassurance. At the end of their assessment, we were told once again that it must just be another ME/CFS symptom. One of the Paramedics told us that his girlfriend had been suffering with ME/CFS for the past three years. It was reassuring to speak to a medical professional who had first-hand experience of the condition. He told us that she had found Shitake Mushroom extract to be particularly helpful. We hadn't tried that so as soon as they left the house I ordered some hoping that as this advice had come from a Paramedic then it would surely work for Jessica. It didn't but I was once again afforded another two weeks of optimism for which I was most grateful.

As mentioned, the colour coding management system requires you to find a baseline - a level of red activity that can be undertaken without payback. Jessica' symptoms were such a muddle by then we didn't know if headaches and stomach pains were payback or due to her periods. Working out what had caused payback when we hadn't expected it ,and whether symptoms were premenstrual or not ,involved us agonising for hours dissecting the day to work out what we had done wrong.

Turns out that finding the baseline is quite a long task. Initially all we could do was guess at where we believed her tolerance was and then slowly keep reducing the time until she did indeed finally not suffer with payback. This took months. And it wasn't even that simple. Different people respond differently to types of energy expenditure. For some, like Jessica, social interaction was exhausting and therefore a red activity. Similarly depending on the severity of the condition, showering and hair washing were red activities. For those less badly affected these activities may be yellow. Working out what your reds and yellows are takes a bit of time but we got there in the end and week on week I completed our charts with pinpoint accuracy. Each hour block was a tiny square of about 1cm x 1cm. To allocate a red activity that lasted five minutes was therefore quite a difficult colouring task. Most of the red activities were a minimum of 20 minutes duration to start with so I managed a third of a centimetre square with a fine tipped pen! It was just the walks that required a magnifying glass to see them.

Our routine was to do a daily walk and then Jessica had to do one of her five minute green times. The walks were our favourite times of the day. To break free from our four walls was an absolute pleasure and we really enjoyed building up our walking time. The principle was to walk for five minutes a day and then increase the time by 20% every 4-5 days. I could never do the Maths but fortunately Jessica has always been good at Maths and we relished those regular increases. We created little loops around our estate, taking a very slightly different route with every added 20%. As we built up the time we gradually managed to walk in to the local town. This felt like a huge achievement and eventually we built up to 30 minutes of walking every day. I suggested that we needed to make one of our walk circuits to pass Jessica's secondary school. She had such traumatic memories of the place that any mention of it or sight of it would really upset her so as we felt we needed to break this pattern, we walked past regularly at a time when we knew all the students would be in class. The more we walked past the more I hoped she would get used to it and slowly rationalise her fears.

The greens that followed the walks however were Jessica's worst times of the day. She would lie in the spare room staring at the ceiling for five minutes. She spent 10 hours a day watching repeat TV to try to distract herself from her pain and thoughts and then had 5 minutes where she was alone with and immersed in them. We stopped this after a while when we knew that it really wasn't helping despite the specialist team's encouragement to keep trying.

Baselines

Jessica recently found three lists she wrote in a diary during her housebound year, the first being 'things that made her happy'. These included reading, getting a letter through the post, listening to music, getting a text (she received very few), baking, and seeing her two best friends. She also wrote of 'reasons I am now afraid of school' which included being seen as 'different' or having special needs; being judged; having questions asked about my health; being asked where I have been; falling behind and being unable to catch up; failing at school; being rejected; having the past repeat itself; not being able to keep up academically and having no friends. The final list was 'things I want to do/have when I am well (be a normal person)' which comprised of taking a long walk in the cold weather; having a day at the beach; having a big family dinner; going to bed late; waking up naturally; eating breakfast; going to a sleepover; being able to dance again; spending a whole day with friends'; eating in a restaurant and going on holiday.

We knew she was struggling with the day to day burden of living with ME/CFS and how she wished for the small things we used to take for granted. For most children her age, wanting to have a family dinner or to get a text are no big deal at all but these were desperately longed for and we all hoped so much that we would start to see progress with the advice from Bath.

We stuck to the programme with rigid determination and it did start to work. We had a wavering but roughly stable baseline, were increasing our daily walks and Jessica was getting to see one of her two best friends for 20 minutes as often as possible. It was very hard to see family or other friends. Any family events were impossible for Jessica and it was hard for us all to miss out on these special occasions. Harder still was seeing Jessica in pain and ill though. We would do anything if it meant getting her well as we could see her resolve, humor and happiness dissolving in front of our eyes.

She was so bored. We were told this was a very positive thing. Being bored is a sign of feeling better physically and we could see this. Rather than being all day on the sofa in pain and exhausted she was starting to be able to do a few things she enjoyed.

One of Jessica's greatest loves is baking. She seems to have a natural talent for it and creates beautiful cakes, biscuits and cookies. We also found it an extremely helpful hobby as it could easily be split into 30 minute slots through the day. I always did the washing up so that she could spend her red time allocation mixing and preparing the batter for the cakes and she rested whilst they cooked and cooled. Later in the day she could then use up another half an hour of red time decorating the cake. She started to take an interest in cake decorating and making fondant animals, flowers and figures. One of our biggest challenges at this point was time management. The thing Jessica needed and wanted most in her life was time with her friends. The girls were fantastic. They understood the Bath system and reliably stuck to the timeframes asked of them to make sure she didn't ever overdo it. This was the highest priority red time and we needed to be sure she had enough scope to see them if they were free. This needed some planning however and it wasn't as easy as just knocking on the door and popping in for twenty minutes as we had to manage her day so carefully.

Jessica's best friends Mum understood how the Bath system worked and was very happy to stick to the rules we had been given to support us. I would keep her updated on the current red time allocation and she would brief her daughter. Jessica resented being able to spend only 20 minutes with her friend so her best friend always came armed with a made up reason why she had to go home after the short time together. None of us wanted her to blame and resent the Bath system as it was making a difference and had stopped the boom and bust we had experienced for so long - her health was relatively stable as long as she managed her time strictly according to the chart. It was absolutely lovely to have two other people help us in this mission as it was tough and 20 minutes fly by when you don't want them to. Everything we did was meticulously planned and implemented.

As with the time spent out walking, other red time was also to be increased by 20% every 4-5 days but she seemed particularly drained by social interaction so we had to slow the increase down to 10% every week. The time slowly crept up in 10% increments until it reached 40 minutes and this felt far better. My friend was an excellent clock-watcher. If we were all together as a family she would keep a close eye on the time and come up with the perfect excuse for the family to depart just at the allotted time. She had always briefed her family in advance and they quickly left the house without Jessica realising quite what planning had gone on behind the scenes to facilitate this short, social interaction. We all have memories of the quickest curry takeaways ever and New Years Eve's where we had to squeeze everything in to the shortest time possible. Once Jessica became a little better we would occasionally go to a pub for dinner with my husband and son driving ahead to get a table and then calling us to read the menu over the phone. Jessica and I would choose our food and once ordered, my husband would wait until the food was being delivered to the table before calling us so we could rush up and eat within the current, allocated time slot. We could only choose pubs very close at hand of course but we all welcomed this venture out as a family so much, and it was on Jessica's list of things she was most looking forward to, it really felt like we were heading in the right direction despite employing such rigid organisational skills. We were very keen that Jessica did not realise the planning involved in everything we did as we knew she would feel really guilty and resent her condition even more. With my friends help and that of my husband and son we managed these covert operations pretty well.

This was probably the thing I hated most, aside from seeing Jessica in so much pain and very unhappy. Anyone that came to the house had a limited time to stay before we needed them to leave. It felt horrible. So rude and unnatural and in the early days the time was so brief they had no sooner arrived than they had to leave. 'Popping in' was the worst. If it hadn't been planned into our allotted red time, it would send Jessica over her red time limit and for sure she would suffer payback for the next four days. We would then have to reduce her baseline again whilst getting back on to an even keel. Living every day minute by minute and continually watching the clock was a daily burden.

Her other very special friend was wonderful. She seemed to have a natural intuition regarding Jessica's feelings and seemed perfectly, and independently, tuned into her friends emotions. She would regularly visit Jessica but understood exactly what our challenges were and arranged times to visit in advance. She was a breath of fresh air as she came in for the short, allocated time. She always had so much to say and such interesting views on life that she and Jessica would chat away until the very last second. She would always get up and leave exactly as agreed and I am so grateful to her for such maturity and empathy in managing the situation. Jessica so looked forward to her visits but the joy was soon over whelmed by the sadness of such a brief respite from her otherwise insular life.

Jessica was managing some home tutoring - a little English and Maths. The school managed to provide a limited amount of tutoring and when that was no longer possible, we found a private Maths tutor. Her lessons were very short to begin with and built up slowly exactly like all other red activities.

It was during this time that we had to go to Hospital for regular check ups. We were fortunate to live only 40 minutes away and have an outreach clinic available, as the service was mostly only accessible from Bath. It was hard for those living with the limiting effects of ME/CFS to have to travel so far for medical appointments. Travelling was an exhausting experience and Jessica always suffered long periods of payback as a result. We both came to resent the time taken for these appointments and dread the days of pain and discomfort that followed. There was little gained from these check up appointments so it felt like we were taking one step forward and two steps backwards all of the time.

The sessions consisted of a brief review of the baseline with both Jessica and I present, followed by half an hour of private counselling where I was asked to leave the room. Jessica disliked these sessions immensely. Due to maternity leave and sickness, the counsellor kept changing and with no time to review notes, the questions asked were frustrating and impersonal. One particular session stuck in Jessica's memory when a new counsellor suggested that she limit the number of sleepovers she had. With only one 20 minute interaction, at home, with one of her two loyal friends, she was a million miles away from a sleepover and it rubbed salt deeply into her growing wounds. A different session was particularly memorable for me when after 15 minutes of slightly bemused discussion the counsellor discovered she had the wrong notes and was actually reviewing a different child altogether.

It was during one of these sessions, that it was recommended that as Jessica was managing 30 minutes of Maths home tutoring, she try to get back in to school for a Maths lesson on those days where it was timetabled for her year group. We set everything up with the Maths teacher, who was incredibly supportive, but jumping from half an hour at home, to an hour in school was way too big a jump. Jessica plummeted from her slowly amassed five hour daily baseline of red activity all the way back to two and a half hours. The ME/CFS term for this is that she 'crashed' – a very appropriate choice of phrase for what was weeks of pain, exhaustion and disappointment. It felt like a game of snakes and ladders. We had just managed to get towards the top half of the board when we slid down the longest snake, right to the very bottom. When she had recovered from the crash we started back at a two-minute walk. The half hour walked we had spent so long accumulating now seemed like a distant goal.

It was some time after this when fortunately, the review appointment and counselling was offered via Skype. I had asked on many occasions whether this would be possible and it seemed that eventually the technology, or funds or whatever else was prohibiting this seemingly essential service, was finally approved. It didn't make the sessions any more worthwhile for Jessica but at least it stopped the payback due to the added journey time.

After every session a report would be written to the school, doctor and paediatrician with an outline of progress. It was never an accurate reflection of the discussion and was the subject of much frustration for me. I never showed them to Jessica so that at least spared her the irritation.

With a baseline now below that with which we had started, attendance at school was impossible. Jessica was too unwell to do any schoolwork for about a year. Most of Year 9 she spent on the sofa feeling very unwell. It was during this time that she started to become nauseous every morning. Jessica would wake every day feeling extremely sick. Sometimes she would be violently sick as she got up and at other times she managed to deep breathe and count to try to stop the feeling welling up inside her. She found this very distressing and started to lose her appetite. She became so frightened that she would be violently sick that she dared not eat and slowly her weight began to drop. The time when she felt 'safe' to eat became later and later. It started at around 10 am and at its worst was nearly 1pm. Even then she ate very little and eventually she was having dinner on a small saucer. Her best friend remembers hugging her thinning frame and noticing her bony fingers commenting on how very fragile she seemed at this time. We all tried very hard not to make a big deal out of her weight and the food she wasn't consuming.

We also had real concerns over her brother. He had started to complain of a lump in his throat all the time. At first we thought it was the result of the end of a cold but it didn't go away and Harvey was becoming distressed by it. We went to the GP and she diagnosed 'Globus Sensation' which is a feeling of having a lump or 'frog' in your throat. We affectionately called it his frog for some while and hoped it would slowly go away. The GP explained that it can be caused by emotional stress and sadly, a while later, there was an episode at school that increased his anxiety to an even higher level. He had been at school eating lunch in the school hall when a child next to him vomited in his dinner. I remember the occasion very clearly as he recounted the tale over and over again with horror over the subsequent weeks. Despite our efforts to make light of it, find an amusing side to the story or distract him, it sunk in deeply and he developed a phobia of vomit. He wouldn't travel on a coach with the school as that was a guaranteed moment for someone to be sick and he started to get highly anxious. On one occasion, I drove him to the Natural History Museum for the school trip so he didn't miss out – we bought a cuddly penguin as a reward for managing to be in such a large public space and keeping calm. It was a challenging day for him and I was relieved that his day went without incident. Needless to say, a child had been sick on the bus on the journey home so we were pleased not to have insisted he travel by coach that day. It would have provided yet more fuel to his growing phobia. The anxiety and phobia began to really affect him and I had discussions with his teachers and football manager so they understood what was going on and could help support him. He had a period of counselling, some hypnotherapy and then I took him to a phobia specialist who taught him some special techniques - eventually these interventions helped and the phobia slowly seemed to dwindle in to the background.

The worst of his phobia however coincided with the worst of Jessica's nausea. Harvey had a severe panic attack one night - I sat on his bed for several hours supporting him, as he tried to breathe deeply and pace around the room to calm himself. We could see what a deep impact Jessica's illness was having on him. On several occasions, my husband and I would look at one another in horror whilst Jessica was being violently sick and our son was suspiciously calling out from his room upstairs to find out what was going on. We made up all sorts of stories and scurried around, one of us rushing off to distract him and the other comforting Jessica whilst rapidly clearing up all evidence. Jessica was frequently sick on the patio outside as she often went out to take deep breaths in the fresh air to try to get the nausea to pass. Indoors, she would have a small, white washing up bowl near to her in case she vomited - the mere sight of this bowl would upset her brother and make him panic.

As Jessica felt increasingly nauseous, she ate less and less and started to lose weight. Her BMI dropped and the Bath team was concerned. I encouraged her to eat as much as possible during the afternoon and evening when the nausea had passed. She was always really keen to eat and was very upset that she was rarely able to keep anything down in the mornings. At the next appointment with the Bath team they weighed her as usual and we discussed her eating habits and the nausea again. Nothing has changed since the last time despite trying to bring her eating time forward by 10 minutes each day as they had suggested. Without explanation two members of staff began talking about 'Jessica's anorexia'. This baffled us both - we didn't believe we were dealing with an eating disorder (Jessica had always loved food and enjoyed cook books and reading about food) but assumed we were just trying to manage one of the many symptoms of ME/CFS. There seemed to be mixed messages about the illness at this stage that we didn't understand. The team wanted us to constantly review her weight and advised that if her BMI dropped any lower she should be taken to hospital to be fed by tube. I was shocked at this comment and couldn't understand why a new diagnosis was being offered out of the blue, as if the ME/CFS couldn't have been to blame.

Since her crash even a two-minute walk was resulting in payback. We had been unable to get Jessica's baseline stable and the payback had returned to its irregular and unfathomable state. We constantly reviewed her activity to see what was causing the payback and where we had gone wrong. Each day something would upset matters and it seemed that even just a few minutes of over doing it would result in days of pain and discomfort. The Bath team suggested that we needed to monitor the amount of walking she did indoors e.g. how many times she walked up the stairs or around the house. The only way to know was to get a pedometer and count her steps. In fact, we ended up with two. One she clipped to her waist and the other to her wrist. They were both so inaccurate. We used the Bath protocols to try to find a baseline number of steps she could do each day and slowly build up by 10% every 4-5 days. Finally, this worked and we started to build steps. The clock watching was continuing but now we were rigidly step counting as well. It was an all-absorbing system and one we had to micro manage due to her seeming intolerance for even a slight misjudgment of red time. At this point, normal activities of daily living had become red time and that made life significantly more difficult.

Time rolled on and we reached the time when every year we booked our annual summer holiday. One of Jessica's annual highlights was searching the internet for houses and choosing the place we would stay that year. This year however felt very different. We knew that Jessica wasn't well enough to travel and she knew it too. She insisted that we go on holiday without her as she knew how much her brother wanted to go and how we all enjoyed our summers away. There was no way we were going without her and explained that we were all content to stay at home. Jessica felt incredibly guilty about this and she was so unhappy we just didn't know what to do for the best.

Around the same time, a friend and colleague who had suffered with ME/CFS for eight years mentioned to me that she found homeopathy significant in getting her back to full health. We had already tried this once before, but we decided it was worth another try and I searched and found another Homoeopath, an ex GP, who specialised in working with people with ME/CFS. We arranged the consultations via Skype and after a thorough review began the treatment. It gave us another new sense of hope as every day and evening we would drop the tincture on to the back of her tongue and watch and wait.

The homeopathy didn't cure Jessica, but it did give us all the confidence to book the holiday that year. We felt in a no-win situation. If we didn't go away, Jessica would feel really guilty about letting us all down and if we did go, she may be ill for a long time with payback. We were very aware of the impact on her brother too - he needed some normality and so after lengthy family discussions, we decided to book. We found a villa in Majorca, not too far from the airport and booked flights from our local airport, just fifteen minutes away. I booked flights at a time that fitted in with Jessica's schedule and made arrangements for assistance at each airport and a wheelchair.

The idea of a wheelchair had been difficult to accept. The first time I knew we needed a wheelchair was when we went on a very quick trip into our local town. Only a five minute drive away, I parked on the square and we walked over to WHSmiths as Jessica wanted to choose a book to read. As we came out of the shop, she almost collapsed, and I had to half carry her back to the car. She was extremely reluctant but even she knew at that point that we needed some help in order to get her out of the house for really brief spells. I hired a wheelchair from the local British Red Cross and it went on a few short excursions. One visit was to a local National Trust property and garden. It was only a very short drive away and we pushed her around for some fresh air – it got us all out of the house for a while and provided a valuable and rare time when we were all out together.

We asked the team at Bath whether it was wise to attempt a family holiday and we were told that if we took measures to manage energy expenditure on route and whilst away, that holidays can be very beneficial for those with ME/CFS. We were told of a family who had just returned with their daughter from a trip to the USA and so we felt reassured that a short flight to Majorca could work out okay for us. Despite my meticulous planning the airline changed the flight times which were nowhere near as convenient or time efficient for Jessica but by that time we were fully committed to the idea and everyone was excited. When the day arrived, we travelled to the airport and were met by friendly and helpful staff. They sat us all together at the back of the aircraft and we encouraged Jessica to go to sleep during the flight as the Bath team had directed. She dozed her way through some of the short flight and we were left on the aircraft until last with one other family who needed assistance. We watched with intrigue as a large vehicle with an elevating ramp appeared at the rear exit and a wheelchair was brought for Jessica to sit in. We toured around some of the less well seen parts of Palma airport and were efficiently passed through passport control. The walk from the terminal building to the car park, where we need to collect the rental car, was very long. I was so grateful that we had arranged for assistance, as Jessica could never have managed the walk. We arrived on the second floor of the car park to collect our hire vehicle which to our surprise was a tiny, two door car. My husband and I looked at our large suitcases and the wheelchair with dismay and spent the next ten minutes discussing how we were ever going to get everything in the car. In the end my son and I sat in the back with a case under our feet and the wheelchair to my side. It was a very uncomfortable journey but we needed the wheelchair to get her back to the terminal building after the holiday so there was no way we were going without it.

The house was lovely with a distant sea view and we made sure Jessica had the best room with double doors facing the view. We managed the holiday as best we could with my husband and I sharing time with each child. We broke the day into the usual 30 minute red times which we shared together and the rest of the time one of us would go out with our son to do some snorkelling or go to the beach or shops, whilst the other stayed with Jessica so she could rest and whittle her time away. It turned out that Spanish yellow time was no better than British yellow time and she spent 50% of her time lying on the sofa watching 'Modern Family' box sets and feeling unwell. I remember her crying as she lay on the small sofa they had in the kitchen and wishing she had never come away as she felt so ill. We did have some good times though – our usual family pool relay races were adapted to piggy back races so that Jessica could just sit on one of our backs and use as little energy up as possible and sitting by the pool during the evening with an ice cream whilst paddling our feet and playing 'the favourite' game as a whole family – it certainly beat just Jessica and I doing it at 3 am in the lounge by ourselves!

That year continued slowly and with little progress. The ups and downs of trying to find a new baseline continued after the holiday although we were pleasantly surprised at the lack of significant payback on return to the UK from Spain.

Aside from our Summer holidays, Jessica's other favourite times of year were birthdays and Christmas. Her love of baking meant Christmas was always full of lovely festive foodie treats. She likes making gingerbread and would decorate biscuits cut in the shape of Christmas trees, stars and hearts with beautiful royal icing pipework. It was a past time that whiled away 30 minutes of red time and she found it relaxing and rewarding.

We hit rock bottom during the Christmas that year. Every family event was tainted with sadness and disappointment, as we knew how much she struggled to cope with social occasions and how ill she would be if she overdid it. That Christmas we tried to engineer the shortest possible family Christmas lunch. I watched the clock endlessly and as time crept on, I became more and more anxious as I could see the colour draining from Jessica's face. She was so polite and never complained but endured the day until everyone left when she crumpled up on the sofa under a blanket with a pounding headache. Boxing day was spent nursing very significant payback and I felt so desperately sad for the plight of our beautiful daughter.

Jessica's best friend was away that Christmas and as we always shared cat feeding duties for one another over holiday periods, the highlight of our Boxing Day that year was spending ten minutes at her house, stroking the cat. I was incredibly thankful for this brief but desperately needed interlude from the confines of our four walls. Her ever thoughtful best friend, had decided to make her a 'things to do' box as a present that year as it is so very difficult to think up and buy presents for someone in Jessica's situation. The handmade box contained bundles of small, coloured envelopes each containing an activity to do when she was either 'bored, very bored, super bored, angry, sad' etc. Of course these activities were carefully thought out to make sure they were yellow in nature (a term used by us all by that point) and included jokes, quick and easy puzzles, cards to make wishes on and quizzes about happy junior school and Stagecoach memories. It certainly provided us with a brief interruption to the drudgery and pain of that day and many others like it and I was incredibly grateful for someone else's yellow ideas. The sad truth about the box that Jessica treasured, and still treasures, is that four of the envelopes had remained unopened until relatively recently. Not because she didn't need them, but because she became so ill that she gave up on life.

January passed and I dreaded the approach of her 15th birthday. Normally a time of such excitement, with plans afoot for days out, presents and happy family gatherings, this year it all felt very different. Jessica had gone from being frustrated and bored with a desperate desire to get her life back, to being resigned to her lonely life on the sofa. She no longer cared, she didn't get upset at not seeing anyone in fact she didn't want to see anyone or go anywhere any longer. She lost all her fight and this was the most worried we ever felt about her. A deep depression seemed to have set in and we could see why. Her 14th birthday had also been a huge disappointment, as she felt really unwell and sat at home all day waiting for the 20 minutes when her best friend popped in with her present. Another friend had promised to pop in but never showed up and that was heart breaking to witness. She loved Nando's at that time and as there was no way she was well enough to go out, my husband drove to collect a takeaway.

By the time it arrived home it was cold and unappetising - a valiant attempt at trying to make the best of the situation but nevertheless a dismal failure.

Birthday's in our house were always marked by a cake. Jessica had become very good creating beautiful fondant novelty cakes. For her 13th birthday she made a cake with fondant figures of her and her best friend sitting on top of a tall iced, chocolate sponge and for her 14th birthday she created a two-tiered, parcel with a label and bow. We have a photo album of the cakes marking every birthday for all members of the family with some amazing creations, my favourite being a basket full of strawberry's that she piped with royal icing for her Aunty's 50th birthday. The photos started with a teddy cake I made for Jessica's 1st birthday and continue for both children to mark every year. As Jessica grew up and developed an interest in baking and decorating I was happily demoted to the washing up and the cakes grew in technical detail. My husband is very creative and joined in these cake highlights of the year too. Such was Jessica's despondency at the turn of her 15th birthday, that she didn't want to create a cake at all. This may not seem that significant to some but in our household this was tragic. I couldn't let her 15th birthday go unmarked in the usual way so hatched a plan to encourage her to bake. She had been toying with the idea of setting up a novelty cake business and we were trying to boost her to do so. I told her that she really needed to practice baking for children's parties and found some gorgeous cake tins that allowed you to make different animals and insects. We chose a ladybird cake, which she reluctantly agreed to bake and decorate with me and conceded to allow this cake to act as her 15th birthday cake. We just couldn't have a void in the photo album for that year.

Trusted Advice

Another family tradition was the birthday breakfast. We treat ourselves to pancakes with maple syrup and bacon, fresh fruit and juices and indulge in this special treat whilst opening presents. We all love piles of parcels.

Jessica's 15th was looming and the nausea finally started to improve. We had spent months and months managing the sickness and nausea and then tried our best to ignore it as we all became used to the daily routine. Jessica desperately wanted to eat a birthday pancake breakfast so each day she tried eating a little something earlier and earlier and to try really hard not to think about nausea. It finally worked and she was as delighted as we were, when her birthday eventually arrived and she was able to tuck in to her favourite breakfast of the year without any side effects.

Around this same time, two key events occurred.

As mentioned, Jessica's mental health had been deteriorating. It was becoming harder and harder to keep her positive and get her to bounce back from the daily upset caused in particular by social media and the sad state of her life. She sat on the sofa and watched as all her friends matured and enjoyed life, posting details of parties they had been to and events they had enjoyed. She shed many tears and regularly deleted her Instagram account as it all became too much to endure. Watching everyone else's lives move on whilst she was stagnating on the sofa, feeling forgotten was a cause of the deepest sorrow.

I was keen to get her back into counselling. Sadly, her two previous attempts had not been a success and this had completely put her off. I had in mind a counsellor whom I had met many years before, as a Pilates client. I had liked her instantly and although we only worked together for six private sessions, she had stuck in my mind. I felt sure Jessica would like her so tracked down her contact details and telephoned to see if she had any vacancies for new clients. Unfortunately, she was fully booked but as I told her our story, she suggested we try the Lightning Process course. Her daughter had also suffered with ME/CFS and got better at age 18 having attended this course. She gave me the contact details of a trainer who ran local courses.

Simultaneously, an acquaintance had made it known that he had also suffered with ME/CFS and had been bed bound for a year. He too had been on the Lightning Process course and fully recovered. We met him one day and he told us of his experience. His father had been a Neurosurgeon and his mother an Optician, so he had grown up in a medical family and following the development of severe ME/CFS his father strongly recommended he attend the course. As a Neurosurgeon, he fully understood the implications of neural plasticity and its relevance in recovery from chronic illness. I remember him clearly saying that he was sure that if he had never attended the course he would still have ME/CFS now.

Knowing and trusting these two individuals I was fully committed to booking Jessica on to the course. I had read about the Lightning Process before and it had mixed reviews. Some said it helped them fully recover, some said it made no difference and some said it made them worse. Without these two personal recommendations, I doubt I would have ever considered it and as the name for the course seemed vague and somehow slightly fake.

I made contact with the local trainer and explained Jessica's situation. The trainer, an ex-dancer who used to run her own dance business, had suffered with ME/CFS for ten years and after meeting the founder of the process, Phil Parker, and going through the training programme herself, had completely recovered. She was so impressed by the science behind it and the technique that she trained to become a Lighting Process coach herself. She explained that before attending Jessica must read the introductory book (An Introduction to the Lightning Process) to explain the science behind it. She then had to complete an application form and have a brief interview to make sure she was suitable for the course. I remember standing outside a local department store when the trainer called me regarding Jessica's application. When she told me that the course was over three days, between 10 am and 1 pm each day my heart sank. Jessica only had three hours of red time available each day and with a forty-minute journey there and back, she would be at risk of serious payback. She told me that we could forget all about clock watching and restricted activity levels – none of this would be relevant after the course. I was really scared as I didn't want to do anything that could potentially make Jessica feel worse but equally the idea that we could forget the charts, pedometers, colour coded activities and clock watching was like a dream come true. With the trust I had in those recommending the process I booked the course during the Easter holidays.

We all read the book. Jessica fully understood the science, which teaches you to learn to reset your body's health systems back to normal by using the well-researched connection that exists between the brain and body. It applies this sound scientific principle so you can get back in charge of three very important processes in the body – The Physical Emergency Response (PER), Allostatic Load and Neuroplasticity. We were fascinated, excited and worried all at once and eagerly anticipated the course with hope once again that this could cure Jessica of ME/CFS.

Jessica had read the book, understood the science and we had committed to the course but the details of exactly what would happen and how, remained a mystery. She was expecting something passive to happen - to be fixed, mended ... like there was a button in your brain that they had discovered to get you well. Her depressive state also meant she was disinterested in the thought of recovery and saw no more reason to try - she had given up by this stage but reluctantly went along with the idea.

Day one of the course we were greeted by the lovely, smiling, cheerful trainer who, alongside another teenage girl and her Mum, took us through to a small consulting room situated in a Chiropractic Clinic. She presented a range of slides to further explain the science behind the process and began to give instructions for the technique. The technique is actually really simple. I was over the moon and so happy that Jessica could be fully empowered to get herself well. We didn't need to see any more medical professionals, try any more medication or colour any more charts – the power to get well was entirely at Jessica's fingertips and I was super motivated to get straight on with it. We were told to go home after the first morning and do something we hadn't done for years. The other girl chose to go on a run with her greyhound and we decided to go shopping together.

As we walked out of the clinic, I was floating on air. I couldn't believe that we could actually go shopping together finally. Something I had dreamed of for so long. Whilst I was beaming from ear to ear, Jessica was the complete opposite.

She cried all the way home. Jessica felt cheated, misled and totally to blame for her illness. Despite all the reassurances, careful explanations and slides of scientific facts to the contrary, Jessica didn't believe it and said she couldn't do it. She found it impossible to accept that a simple technique was the cure for all the pain and suffering she had endured for so long. I was desperate. I pleaded with her to do the techniques. We both believed in the science and yet she wasn't prepared to try and she was so angry. We finally sulked our way around the shopping centre, with Jessica practicing the techniques through gritted teeth at my insistence and eventually made it home with the prospect of not going back for day two.

I had run out of things to say and ways to make her see the course in a positive light so my husband took her out for a drive. They sat in the car near a local beauty spot in the countryside and talked for ages. My husband's calm and gently persistent manner began to encourage Jessica and make her see what an opportunity this was, that there was no blame and she was most certainly not at fault. I sat at home holding my breath and hoping he had managed to persuade her to continue the course. When they walked back through the front door and told me we were going to the second day I was extremely relieved.

Day two comprised of more science and further practice of the techniques. Jessica had no signs of payback. We were sent home with a further mission to do something we had dreamed of doing for a long time. We drove to the beach, met my son and husband and had a fantastic time at the arcade. We had fun, all together and I never looked at the clock once. It felt like being set free.

Day three comprised of more science and further practice of the technique. Jessica still had no obvious payback and we had done more activity than she had done in years. That evening we came home, packed our bags and went away for the weekend to a small hotel which we had been to and loved years before. We went swimming at the hotel, went out for dinner and after a long walk at the beach climbed to the very top of a cliff and had a group hug overlooking the bay. We all felt on top of the world, except for Jessica.

The incredible freedom we had suddenly been given was like a dream come true. When we returned from the weekend away, we all decided that it would be great to do a long walk in the countryside. I had heard of a local, organic farm shop and cafe and we thought it would be nice to walk there and back. I explained the location to my husband and we set off on a beautiful sunny day following him as he confidently guided us along a quiet footpath. Turns out the place he thought we were going to and the place I had intended we went were quite different and instead of walking two to three miles we ended up walking ten. We were all exhausted by the time we finally arrived at the cafe and relished a drink and break. We discussed calling my Mum or sister to rescue us and take us home but in the end my husband found a shortcut home and he persuaded us all to walk. To think that only a week before Jessica had been trapped within the boundaries of less than three hours in total of red time, broken into half an hour slots through the day, seemed incomprehensible.

Outwardly, Jessica was coping and from the moment we attended the course we never witnessed any more payback. We believed she was doing the techniques in her own way but in fact, her version of the process meant inwardly she was being incredibly hard on herself. She carried a self-perceived blame around with her constantly and although accurately enforced some key concepts from the course, those that would have underpinned greater self-confidence, forgiveness and self-compassion were omitted. Every day she mentally battled her own way out of the ME/CFS symptoms in the harshest way.

To the rest of us we delighted in the fact that she was finally cured. And yet the aftermath and fallout of the illness and her recovery was still a huge challenge. The pacing protocols had left her isolated and feeling that she couldn't do things and the course had left her feeling to blame for ever having become ill.

Unravelling Past Experiences

Jessica was left with a mass of emotion. She had the green light to live again but needed a slow and progressive reintroduction to life. She had nothing to go back to - no structure, few friends and no desire to live. The thought of reintegrating into the world was frightening and, in some ways, although for years we had all felt desperate for a way out, we had become slightly accustomed to the way things were and had reached a level of acceptance of the truth of this restricted existence. One has to come to some form of peace with it all to cope with the everyday and now all of a sudden Jessica was scared of stepping out of this safe zone. She wasn't just scared though …. by now Jessica was at the stage of feeling suicidal.

Several significant people entered our lives around this time. Following the year of total absence from school, the Special Needs Coordinator applied for a statement of ill health that allowed her to qualify for one hour of home tutoring a day. This process had been arduous. We had to defend Jessica's ill health at a meeting in the Head teacher's office with numerous parties involved in receiving this educational support. We were threatened with Ofsted visits to our home and although we knew they were trying to help they made us feel intimidated, judged and uncomfortable. Our home had to be risk assessed and there was a brash and harsh approach, which seemed so unnecessary at the time. The process was entirely defensible; the approach was hard to swallow.

Still, we were incredibly grateful when we were finally granted the hour a day of tutor support for English and Maths that Jessica so deserved. I waited with fear and trepidation on the first day that the new English tutor was due at the house. Jessica and I greeted her at the door and I left them both in the kitchen whilst I sat in the next room with half an ear on what they were speaking about. I was keeping everything crossed that she would be a kind person. The tutor sat down, opened her laptop and started to talk to Jessica about her interests and hobbies and showed her photographs of her horse and dog. It was the perfect start. She asked Jessica all about the things that she loved (favourite books, characters, films etc.) and they spent a long time just getting to know one another. They both loved animals and baking and immediately developed a rapport which was the most important first step for our daughter. The task of trying to catch up on all she had missed in GCSE English Language and Literature was daunting but the tutor took everything a step at a time and really supported Jessica with a deep empathy, genuine kindness and patient approach. As soon as the tutor left after that first meeting, Jessica beamed. She liked her very much indeed and their relationship was off to a wonderful start.

I had the exact same feelings when the Maths tutor knocked on the door the next day. Again, my overriding hope was that she was kind. And she most certainly was. The Maths tutor was gentle, patient and thoughtful. She explained everything so clearly to Jessica - there was no pressure, no tests – just a gradual explanation of concepts and total support of her needs. As we closed the door to her we had a hug of sheer joy that we had the support of these two wonderful ladies to take Jessica through her GCSE's.

At first Jessica could only manage 40 minutes of tutor time. She had one year until the exams and didn't have the capacity to add in any additional self-study. Jessica continually told us during this time that she was 'not clever anymore'. She had always been academic, hardworking and bright but after such a long absence from her studies, she was petrified that she would never be able to make up lost time and would fail her exams. She had regular panic attacks before the arrival of the tutors and would often appear with red eyes having just about pulled herself together.

They never said a word. They just smiled, took their time and carried on. With their support, Jessica gradually started to make headway and we found it quite remarkable what good progress could be made with one-to-one attention. The tutors slowly filled the gaps in Jessica's knowledge without making her feel that she was stupid, which was exactly what we needed to get her back on an educational path. Slowly and step by step she increased the time per session until she reached the maximum of one hour that was provided. She could however then begin to add personal study time, which we increased very slowly and finally she started to achieve more and more.

Everyday however, Jessica was overwhelmed by feelings of defeat. My husband and I would share the daily task of trying to get her to see her situation more positively. As the perceptions of herself were by now significantly damaged, this was no easy task and we would work together to start each new day boosting what the other had told her the day before, hoping for a change in her beliefs so that she could see the reality of what we saw. We knew she was doing incredibly well but Jessica always compared herself to her friends and she was a long way away from the reality of their situations.

Her tutors never graded Jessica's work. She was always told that the work was good and her efforts were valued. This was exceptionally helpful. Not to be labelled or to feel that your self-worth was linked to a grade (a letter or number) was such a refreshing and essential part of Jessica's recovery.

We were all delighted that she was making progress and Jessica was determined to try to get her studies back on track as soon as she could. Although there was no more funding for additional subjects, the Maths tutor fortunately also tutored Science, so we paid for extra lessons when she was up to it. This allowed a glimmer of optimism that she might indeed be able to gain entry to college with a possible five GCSE's including English and Maths. It continued to be tough psychologically as Jessica continued to compare herself to her peer group. They were busy with up to twelve GCSE's and getting involved in Duke of Edinburgh award schemes and other extracurricular activities. It seemed that for every giant step forward Jessica made, it paled into insignificance when compared to what everyone else was doing. This became the focus of our support to her every day. We reassured her that she wouldn't be behind for long, that once the GCSE's were over she would be at college and back on an even playing field with her peers once more and that her illness didn't need to define her as a person any longer. She could get back to being the Jessica she was before and forget all about ME/CFS. We had many discussions about GCSE grades and desperately wanted her to be happy with whatever results she achieved because she was trying to catch up on years of missed input. Needless to say, that wasn't okay with Jessica. She needed to perform at her old standards, or she would be incredibly unhappy with herself. Her self-loathing and lack of confidence was by now firmly rooted and the years of illness, misdiagnosis and poor management needed a massive effort to unravel.

Her godmother had been a constant support throughout Jessica's illness. Always just a phone call away with irregular and yet impeccable timing, she would seem to call just when I needed a chat most. She was always generous in her time and so understanding - she most certainly understood what we were all going through. As a drama teacher she had taught Verse and Prose LAMDA exams to children for many years and as she lived a long distance away offered to do weekly Skype lessons with Jessica so that she could take her Grade 5 exam. In her younger, well years, Jessica had worked her way through LAMDA acting exams and it had been yet another loss when she was too unwell to continue. Her godmother's kind offer was a perfect way for Jessica to gently feel that she could achieve again. They enjoyed one another's company each week and she prepared for an exam at a local public centre. It was the first exam she had taken since her illness and I was keen that she faced the inevitable anxiety of such a situation before her GCSE's. Jessica passed with flying colours which was a well needed boost and a process that reacquainted her with coping with the general pressures of life.

As much as situations like that boosted her confidence, social media constantly damaged her self-confidence. By Year 11, all her friends were becoming independent, making their own plans and beginning to experience more of life as they headed towards adulthood - there were multiple events that Jessica was missing out on and her feelings of isolation deepened. The only event Jessica could participate in was a teenage market, run at at local village hall where she and three friends had a cake stall. Jessica was helped by her Grandma and Aunty to bake a selection of tray bakes, cakes, muffins, cookies and cupcakes. They raised a pleasing amount of money, which they split between the Action for ME charity and another charity personally linked to a relative of one of Jessica's friends. We were so very pleased to finally see her participating with her friends in this way although the event just reinforced Jessica's feelings of the huge gap she still had to cross.

Around a similar time, her two friends were preparing to travel to Kenya with the school to do charity work for a local school near Nairobi. At that time Jessica would have loved to do this trip but as she could not attend she watched and listened from the sidelines. We knew Jessica needed something to make her feel like she was a part of this exceptional experience and baking came to the rescue.

With my husband's help she designed and developed a website to sell cakes, in particular novelty cakes for special occasions. Her experience gained over many years creating birthday cakes, meant she had a lots of cake photographs for the site and once shared, family and friends were generous with their orders. For every cake made, Jessica donated all of her time and effort, and we donated the ingredient costs, to her friends fundraising cause for the Kenya trip. In total she raised approximately £600 and this allowed her to feel that she played her own part in the adventure her friends were about to embark upon.

Her love of cake baking, and success with cake orders, led us to enroll her for decorating classes on a Tuesday afternoon. We were told of a retired lady who ran classes at her home nearby and she was very happy to work with Jessica once a week. She showed Jessica how to create some amazing effects with royal and fondant icing. It was another small step forward to getting her out of the house and learning something new that she enjoyed.

Getting out of the house was a daunting task for someone who has been so rigidly housebound for so long and the effect on Jessica's self-confidence was profound. The structured, controlled steps forward, like the weekly cake classes, were wonderful and started a spiral upwards but she needed confidence to start to get out into the world by herself again. Her experience with ME/CFS had completely cut her off from life and we were starting from rock bottom. This is when we welcomed a new addition to our family.

For many years my husband and the children had wanted us to have a dog but I was always reluctant. Never a dog lover, following years of living next door to an intimidating Alsatian dog when I was young (which would leap at our fence, snarl and bark every time my sister and I went into the garden) I had always preferred cats and in fact had no deep desires for any pet at all. We talked about it for a long time and eventually decided that if ever there was ever going to be a good time for us to have a dog, it would be then. We found a breeder who had one puppy left for collection at the end of August and we snapped him up. A beautiful cream and apricot bundle of fluff with whom we all immediately fell in love. Our Cavapoo came in to the family and brought immediate joy and life to the house. Jessica was still studying at home and was able to walk him every day; keeping her active and increasing her time walking to begin to regain some normal levels of physical fitness. He was a fun and reassuring walking partner and although at this stage Jessica had severe social anxiety, she started to chat to other people walking their dogs and develop a rapport with local dogs and their owners. Just that daily interface with other adults and the joy of watching the dogs run and play together, made a significant difference to her overall health and confidence. It was one of the best decisions we ever made and he has provided endless cuddles, exercise, giggles and holidays … each of these building back a small part of the Jessica that had been lost.

However, not all decisions were quite that good and despite admirable and brave enthusiasm, one endeavor did not have such a positive outcome. Such was Jessica's desire to get back to normal and do what every other teenager was doing; she decided to enroll in the National Citizenship Service (NCS). This was a government-funded scheme for young people in the UK to go away from home for several weeks and take part in charitable works, experience new activities and learn/develop as a preparation for further studies/adulthood. The marketing was very good and the staff and lectures/information evenings were well run and informative. Although Jessica was highly anxious, she was also determined to step out of her safety zone and get back to normal with people of her own age. She had spent a great deal of time with adults but now she was well, she needed to socialise with her peers again. We packed and prepared for her first week of activities, which was to be held in Cornwall. Jessica knew no-one else on the trip and was reassured by the marketing that led us to believe that everyone would be in the same position, and it was time to make new friends. I fully informed the staff of her background, that she had just recovered from ME/CFS and suffered with high levels of anxiety requiring additional support. She filled in an application form and ticked most of the mental health issues mentioned which was sent to the enrolment team and we were reassured that all her needs would be met. The day arrived when I dropped Jessica at a local sports ground for the coach journey to Cornwall. There were hundreds of teenagers at this location; all being placed into different locations for various expeditions and it was overwhelming for her. Despite the tears and anxiety however, she insisted on going and I drove away feeling concerned but hopeful that this may be a huge milestone for her social reintegration. Sadly, the additional support that Jessica needed to cope in such an environment was not forthcoming. Her group comprised of several players from the same football team and all of the girls went to the same school. The adult in charge was no more than a couple of years older than Jessica, unprepared and ill equipped to know how to deal someone with high levels of anxiety. Despite lengthy form filling and discussions with senior members of staff, promises that were made were not kept and my husband ended up driving four hours to a Cornish campsite at 2 am after Jessica called having a panic attack. She was so relieved to be coming back home after her brief but tortuous stay and felt demoralised at the failure of her attempt. To us however it was a remarkable achievement. To go from being alone at home for such a long period, to having the courage to travel a long way from home with a group of people she had never met was a giant leap forward and despite Jessica's already deeply ingrained self-loathing, even she could see (after hours of discussion) quite what an accomplishment this was. She also made a friend who she kept in contact with for several years afterwards.

The self-loathing was a prolonged and difficult result of her illness. In Jessica's case the treatment and eventual cure both reinforced her feelings of hatred toward herself. To have been given a treatment plan that isolated her and ingrained the psychology of being 'unable to do things' slowly ate away at her confidence and ironically as her physical health improved and symptoms subsided, her head space was full of negative and damning inner thoughts. She felt useless, lost, worthless and pointless. The Lightning Process couldn't undo the past four years and although she had her physical abilities back she didn't have her life back. Jessica described the year, post Lightning Process, as the most difficult time of the whole experience. Becoming ill, being in severe pain and incapacitated all pale into insignificance when faced with the uphill struggle to get back socially and psychologically to where you should have been all along. One of the challenges was differentiating between being what we called 'ME tired' and 'normal tired'. Everyone feels tired, but Jessica had no way of recognising whether her feeling was now just what everyone else felt or memories of payback. It took a long time to slowly ease back into feeling okay about being tired and we all bizarrely avoided the subject for fear of it being a trigger or upsetting her.

It was our mission to rebuild Jessica's confidence and start to pick up all the pieces that had been left behind. Several events were very helpful during this time.

My sister kindly offered Jessica some work experience at her pre-school where she went in once a week to do baking with the children. My Mum and I would drop her off and go for a walk with the dog whilst she spent the morning playing in the sand pit with them, singing and dancing, drawing and reading and making cookies, biscuits and cakes. It offered her a safe environment in which to have faith in herself once again, to do something positive and rewarding and make relationships with those outside of the family. She also worked at a local cake shop working as a decorator and serving in their small café. The owners of the shop liked Jessica very much and she was diligent, professional and reliable. It was a huge boost to her when at the end of the Summer, they offered her an apprenticeship to work with them and develop their business.

These affirmations of her worth were invaluable and every one of them notched her another small step forwards. To hear and receive news like this at home was priceless. We had waited so long and coped with years of a downward spiral that to feel upwards momentum was bliss. We knew there was a long way to go, but we celebrated every step of the way.

There is nothing like external ratification of worth. As parents, you can constantly praise, reassure and encourage but in our case, our words were always slightly devalued as Jessica knew how much we loved her and that our love was totally unconditional. In her eyes we would of course say anything to make her feel better even if it wasn't true. To have an adult outside of the family unit offer praise and attestation of significance was like gold dust. We rejoiced at each comment. Higher rated still was praise from her peers.

Jessica finished off the summer holidays with a Skydive alongside my husband and two close friends. We waited for their jump all day as the cloud cover was thicker than anticipated but at the last minute a break appeared in the clouds and they all took off in the little rickety plane with their tandem dive partners. Jessica's only comment when she landed was how cold it was. With little self-praise or 'well done me' moments (something we worked very hard on with her over those post ME/CFS years) she said that she would rather jump out of a plane any day than face college with 1500 teenagers. Teenagers and her future were her biggest fear.

With college looming and the clock ticking to make decisions about A level choices and possible University courses, we were delighted when at last the counsellor had availability to take Jessica on as a new client. For a long time, every time we mentioned college or prompted discussions about her future Jessica would have a panic attack and we knew that we had done and were doing all that was in our power to help her psychologically, but she needed professional help to move forwards (and someone external to us to allow her to see the real truths about what an amazing person she was).

Jessica and I had an opening session with the counsellor where we tried to summarise the events of the past four years and her current state of mental and physical health. Having a daughter who had ME herself, she knew only too well the realities of the illness, prejudices and controversy over the condition and techniques of the Lightning Process, so a great deal didn't need to be explained. This was invaluable as we had no worries over her not 'getting it' and after years of coping with the majority of people who really don't understand, this special lady was a true gift. They developed an immediate rapport and worked together over the next two years with slow and steady progress. Jessica would make notes each week of everything she needed help with to steer her sessions and for a long time the advent of a Wednesday evening was desperately craved. Every week the rocky events of the past seven days would be unraveled and Jessica was put back on an even keel. The difference in her during that hour was palpable and it was a tremendous relief to us that we had Jessica's wellbeing in such safe and experienced hands.

One of the biggest issues to tackle was Jessica's dislike of herself, both physically and mentally. She hated her thoughts, actions and how she looked and would spend long periods of time watching YouTube video blogs of teenagers with depression, anxiety and various psychological disorders. One such teenage girl had a disorder called Trichotillomania – a type of impulse control disorder where individuals will pull out their hair when stressed to soothe themselves. For a long time, Jessica would watch the videos and feel a deep empathy with these individuals all of whom were going through a similar psychological and physical torment as her. Despite our suggestions of their unhelpfulness, she was absorbed by a form of comfort it gave her that she was not alone and there were other people suffering like she was. Her two close friends were flourishing and life for every teenager she knew, looked from the outside to be going to plan, with adventures, social joys and new experiences being posted on Facebook, Instagram, Snapchat and other social media. Jessica felt that she was different – something she hated with a deep-rooted passion. For every picture and post of confident, happy and achieving friends, Jessica's self-loathing increased and although she never once wished ill of anyone else, she was sinking deeper and deeper in to a dark personal place. Finally, one day Jessica realised that watching these videos were causing her harm and actually not providing real comfort at all. This sudden opening of her eyes was such a relief and from that moment, she did not spend any more time entertaining negative influences that weren't beneficial to her own mental health.

We continued to back up the work Jessica did with the counsellor and mainly focused our attentions on the previously mentioned 'well done me' moments in her life. Finally, after so long, she was now doing things, we had ample opportunity to highlight and reinforce the progress she had made and how significant every step was, even if it may have only seemed like a small step for someone else. Countless dog walks were full of long discussions to help her see quite how remarkable her achievements were. The subject that probably notched up the most hours of discussion was that of her likely GCSE results.

Jessica had never sat an exam, missed three quarters of her schooling and struggled through anxiety and depression and recovered from a condition that is little understood, widely belittled and stigmatised and yet she was catching up academically. She never believed this however, and despite both her tutors praise, genuine admiration and support she always doubted her abilities. During her early secondary school years there was constant pressure not to drop a grade and rather than providing the much needed message of 'your health is most important, don't worry you can catch up later when you are well' the message was 'get in to school even if you are ill, unable to cope, anxious and behind because your grades matter most'. This constant barrage of input from a revered source was incredibly difficult to break through and we didn't succeed at that stage to get through to her.

Thankfully the school arranged for all her GCSE exams to be sat at home with an invigilator. The careers advisor at the school was a bubbly, optimistic lady who was full of life and energy and was given the role to sit with Jessica whilst she undertook her exams. She provided a much needed, calming influence at the beginning of each exam and Jessica coped admirably, even pulling herself around from a panic attack just a few minutes before the English exam started. The wait for results was of course a long one and seems interminable for every GCSE student and their parents, but for us so much rested on these results. We had been unable to break through that psychological barrier that her worth as a person didn't relate to her results and desperately hoped she would do well as that was the only way she could ever genuinely be able to be proud of herself. ME/CFS had taken away a quarter of her life and she resented it deeply. If she failed her exams, it would have been a blow so great, we weren't sure she would ever recover from it.

On the morning of the exams, her friends were all going in to school together to pick up their results. Jessica didn't want to see any other pupils at the school so we walked together as late as we could to miss the rush and avoid as many people as possible. Jessica bravely walked into the school (a significant moment as she had very bad memories of the place) and was greeted by the careers lady who had been waiting patiently for hours for her to arrive. She knew the results and desperately wanted Jessica to open the brown envelope with her friends but there was no way Jessica was prepared to risk that. Instead she gathered up her envelope and together with the careers lady walked outside to the pavement opposite where I was waiting with our dog. I held my breath as she opened the envelope and saw tears run down her face and then thank goodness saw a smile appear. All three of us hugged and cried at this momentous occasion. She had done superbly well and at that moment even Jessica couldn't possibly fail to see that a 'well done me' moment was in order.

The panic attacks continued as we considered options for her future. Despite achieving outstanding results, she was terrified of college – not of the workload but of the teenagers within. The careers lady at the school kindly introduced her to the special need's coordinator at the college and between them they arranged for private tours of the college so Jessica could avoid the open evening and crowds of people. Both ladies were so kind and genuine – they gave me a feeling of complete trust that they would support Jessica fully and help her just as I would. This feeling was rare. On far too many occasions whilst Jessica was becoming ill (and then throughout her illness) we were surrounded by disbelieving and judgmental people. This was a very sad reality of the condition, but it proved to highlight those very special individuals to whom we are incredibly grateful. I think they all know who they are and without them we may not be able to sit here today and feel so grateful that we have a daughter who has now fully recovered, not only physically but now finally also psychologically and socially.

The early days of her recovery were surprisingly difficult for everyone, particularly for her best friend, who was so used to looking out for signs and symptoms that Jessica was over doing things. She and I would see a look come over Jessica, particularly in her eyes, when she started to feel unwell and by then we all had little habits and routines that we subconsciously carried out to keep her safe and as well as possible. Heat, bright lights and noise were such an issue during her illness and the few of us that were very close to her every day would eventually instinctively assess environments and try to make them as comfortable as possible for her, opening windows, turning down heating, dimming lights etc. On one occasion the girls were celebrating a day out at a theme park, enjoying all the rides and reminiscing about the many happy days we had all spent there when they were young, and her best friend remarked how hard it was on that day not to look out for those familiar signs. She was so used to observing Jessica and asking if she was okay or needed a break and all of a sudden she just didn't need to do that anymore. Her Mum was the same. We smiled when she would drift back into habitual Jessica management practises, which had been the norm for so long, and I would have to remind her, and me, that we didn't need to hang on to any tiny fragment of ME/CFS any longer. As the Lightning Process had taught us, it needed letting go completely in the confident knowledge that it would never come back. It was an amazing relief.

Jessica often delved deeply to find her inner strength and amazed us with some courageous actions, the most memorable of which was her school awards ceremony. Jessica had been officially dual schooled when she left mainstream education and was still eligible to take part in the GCSE awards which were held in the school hall. She still had a real fear of the building and people within it and by choice would have avoided any further contact with the school. However, we gently encouraged her to reconsider as her results had been so outstanding we felt she deserved as much recognition and praise as possible and of course we wanted her to create some new positive memories of the place. The evening was formal with parents, students and teachers in attendance and the head of year called each tutor group up to the stage in turn to shake their hand and receive their award. Most tutor groups comprised of ten or so students and they all gathered in their groups to prepare to be called to the stage. Jessica stood all alone - the one and only, solitary member of the IU tutor group. The head of year called the IU tutor group first and I saw a look of terror pass over Jessica's face as she realised she was not only alone but the first to receive her award. She bravely walked up the steps to the stage, smiled and shook the teacher's hand to a round of applause and made it back to her seat, having outwardly oozed quiet confidence. We knew she was petrified but she never showed it and my husband and I were so incredibly proud of her.

Conclusions

We had many happy, normal years during Jessica's early childhood and until she was aged nine. Very pleasurable memories of great times and busy lives that we took for granted - we never dreamt we would be faced with something as life changing as this to cope with. It is easy to overlook everyday pleasures and forget to be grateful for the small things but one positive I have certainly drawn from those horrible four years is a heightened awareness of how good normal is. It has taken on a new and amazing quality and I strive to remind myself of this. That's one thing I don't ever want to lose sight of as the memories of 2012-2016 gradually, and happily fade.

I had read some stories of those who had recovered from ME/CFS but mostly my research led me to stories of the harsh reality of the severe symptoms associated with the condition and those still deeply distressed whilst trying to exist within its limitations. The sad truth of many an individual's story is one of hopelessness and a complete lack of direction toward feeling trustful of a recovery. Delirious in one's desire for that chance to get better so many of us have floundered from one 'cure' to another - some options perfectly logical, some less mainstream and all of them feeling like you are grasping at straws. The world outside of ME/CFS needs to understand this disorder and the very real physical and psychological suffering that goes on behind closed doors. It is shocking to witness the severity of the symptoms and you do feel this desperate need to bring the reality of the pain and suffering into the vision of those with disbelieving eyes.

Some years after Jessica's recovery we found out that a pupil in her class had been spreading rumours about her. She told other pupils at the school that Jessica was making up her illness for attention and her mother had informed other parents that I was making up fake symptoms to make it look as though she was sick. I was tremendously grateful neither of us knew this at the time and was disappointed to learn that her mother, whom I often met at the local supermarket and would share a short discussion about Jessica's health, had in fact been the source of such unkind rumors.

It is astonishing to think that we are still mystified by this condition after so many years and to acknowledge that Medical Science still seems to have no definitive answers. In our experience, most people are critical, suspicious and cynical, few are compassionate and empathetic. Specialist support remains inaccessible for many and despite those few within the medical profession who have diligently and tirelessly worked for a mainstream treatment plan, the wheels of progress are far too slow and, in the end, the current interventions, once finally received, are inadequate and in some instances may be more damaging than helpful.

Looking back, Jessica's ME/CFS started so slowly it is difficult to pinpoint an exact start date for the onset. The assortment of issues occurring at the time made any clarity over her symptoms impossible. Although the pacing programme made a difference to her health and allowed her to feel more well again, it had taken away her life and she seemed sentenced to this unendingly, micromanaged world where she was afraid to laugh too much for fear that she would exceed her energy limitations of the day and sink back into payback. I remember an occasion when Jessica was with her friend for that limited half an hour slot and they were baking and giggling as they put on some music and started to dance. I was filled with horror and fear that she was overdoing it and was desperate for them to be calm and quiet and sit down. That can't be right. That's not living.

We are grateful to the Lightning Process as we were given new information, a set of tools to use and assurances, backed by medical science, that she would be able to live life to the full again. Many others never consider themselves fully recovered, either still suffering the symptoms or somewhere in their psyche hanging on to the thought that it may return, or it never actually went away. Nevertheless, it left Jessica with many other issues to tackle, and it is easy to see how her perspective on the matter led her to draw the conclusions she did.

Our experience of ME/CFS is completely unique as is that of every other person who has ever suffered or is still suffering with this illness. Everyone has a different onset, set of symptoms, level of severity and differing personality traits and characteristics creating an unfathomable number of variables to manage. Unanimously however, we share the desire to know what this disorder is and how to get better. As confusion and misdiagnoses thrive, the clock ticks and one's life is slowly chipped away, every day digging an individual deeper into the grasps of the condition and its side effects. Rapid diagnosis and prompt, appropriate advice is critical in addressing and resolving the cause of the illness patterns, not just attempting to relieve the symptoms. My husband and I still do not know what advice we would give to another suffer of ME/CFS - after all our experiences and knowledge on the subject we still have no real answers and trying to recommend a course of action for another individual with unique needs seems impossible.

Following the emergence of Covid-19 and the now recognised phenomena of Long Covid which resembles ME/CFS in almost every way (except the issues with breathing difficulties which are clearly representative of that particular virus) it would be reasonable to hope that joint funding for these conditions could now be found. Maybe one and the same illness, so many would benefit from better diagnosis, clearer treatment protocols and being cared for as a whole person - the biological, social and psychological aspects need addressing at the same time to create successful outcomes.

Jessica completed a Biomedical Sciences honors degree in 2022 and her chosen dissertation was entitled 'The Immunopathological similarities between Long Covid and ME/CFS and its wider implications'. Although her research was purely related to the biomedical side of the illnesses and therefore deals specifically with the immune response, her view of future care is the same as mine. Looking at the condition and its effect on the whole person must be addressed.

Her concluding dissertation remarks are as follows:

"The immune responses to both viruses leading to the development of the same chronic symptoms have many overall similarities, but many questions remain. Most of the parallels observed are superficial and have yet to be analysed, therefore the correlations cannot be confused for causations. However, the striking number of similarities gives a launch point for further research in the immunopathological similarities of Long-COVID and ME/CFS. As ME/CFS can be trigged by many different viruses and physical trauma resulting in the complex array of symptoms seen among patients, I believe that 'Long-COVID 'should be included under the umbrella of ME/CFS, acknowledging that this variation that has been triggered by COVID infection. Now that a vast number of individuals are suffering from post-viral Covid syndrome due to the pandemic, if Long-COVID were to be classed as a type of ME/CFS this would greatly benefit those suffering with ME/CFS that have been cast aside for decades. I would estimate that research and clinical trials would be conducted in higher volume, and current understandings could be re-evaluated to improve the treatment of both cohorts"

I'm often asked what ME/CFS is - interestingly this is exactly the question Jessica was asked by her two professors during questions at her dissertation presentation. Neither one had ever heard of it.

My thoughts are as follows; I believe that ME/CFS is an overload reaction following an initial illness or trauma (some stressor to the bodies systems and a trigger out of wellness - in Jessica's case Glandular Fever) that is prolonged to the point where the body/mind get set on an illness Autopilot. Modern life does not allow an individual the time or means to get properly better from such serious viruses, conditions or traumas and rushes them before their bodies are ready to do so, further stressing the Sympathetic Nervous System and closing down the healing Parasympathetic Nervous Response. Society knows and accepts the best route to recovery from a broken bone but unless there is something visible we seem blind to the similarities. The overwhelmed sufferer struggles to cope with the cumulative burden of chronic stress and symptoms worsen. As the condition takes hold over time, the brain becomes stuck in this pattern of illness and sets itself on repeat having triggered a series of symptomatic, protective bodily responses. Each person experiences this differently representing their own individual view of the world and the complex set of contexts and emotions concerned. This Autopilot setting is completely subconscious and results in a multitude of disabling and unpleasant symptoms. Time, detachment and rest allow the body to start to rebalance, but to confidently fully recover some defining moment has to occur to shift the brain out of its negative spiral into a positive one and unlock the body from its incarceration. This may be a course such as we experienced or eventual actions through an inspirational route that delivers true belief to the individual that control can be regained, and life can be lived again. The true challenge is time. A shift in thought pattern, a moment of self-established clarity and slow steady physical progress can take years to develop in order to create an environment for change and wellness. This is time the ME/CFS sufferer cannot afford to spend without creating a wealth of adverse ill effects. Like a relentless and unstoppable seesaw, the progress of time served with this condition produces further physical and psychological harm.

I have met and been in contact with a few other Mums' just like me who have all had daughters blighted by this condition. Each have their own story to tell, very different to ours and yet similar in so many ways. All had to reluctantly remove themselves from the day-to-day pressures of life and seek rest. As if belonging to some undesirable club, we have shared and witnessed the familiar signs and symptoms of this condition and been able to play a small part in supporting each other during dark times. Each one of us has been grateful for an email or phone call when things were tough, and we didn't know where to turn next and sharing experiences was a lifeline along the way. Likewise, I have the pleasure of knowing several other amazing individuals who have also experienced this condition and are now living normal lives. Sharing their stories has been tremendously helpful in placing our experience in a wider context.

I hope this account of Jessica's journey highlights the experience as a whole. This is not just looking at one symptom or a small part of the journey, it is about appreciating the condition and its effects in its entirety, right from the beginning until the very end, effects that are both physical and psychological in nature. The ongoing debate of whether ME/CFS is either a physical or psychological condition must be overcome. Progress doesn't need to take sides and psychological health doesn't need to be stigmatised. The brain and the body don't work independently and this illness highlights above anything else the constant interaction between the two and that continual criss-crossing of pathways.

It is a sad fact that some of those researching this condition have had to stop their work due to the aggressive behaviour of certain individuals. I do understand this anger. The treatment of anyone with this condition is so poor that it can so easily lead to a pathway of frustration, disillusionment and hostility. Those who vehemently believe this is a psychosomatic disorder versus those who believe it is a purely physical condition. The battle of the two sides is unhelpful at best and totally damaging at worst.

There appear to be many overlapping conditions - Fibromyalgia and Chronic Regional Pain Syndrome being the two I have been most closely associated with via clients, family, colleagues and friends. Jessica and I prefer to use the term ME for her illness as Chronic Fatigue Syndrome doesn't accurately reflect her experience, although it is relevant for others who have debilitating fatigue as a primary symptom. Jessica's main symptom was systemic pain and I always consider her experience to be better described as Chronic Pain Syndrome. Where the overlap between the other conditions mentioned seems confused, ultimately all seem to have the same root priority - rapid diagnosis and prompt, appropriate and personalised advice. We seem a long way from this sadly and with the time that passes the chances of secondary health issues and psychological trauma increase dramatically making recovery a long and complex task.

My final comment must of course be directed at our courageous, talented and considerate daughter who has endured so much and is thriving once more. I remember having to fill in a form when the Special Needs Co-ordinator at her Secondary School applied for a statement of ill health, and there was a box asking for a description of characteristics of the child concerned: my first word was brave. The teacher looked confused and asked why I had written this word on the form – after all, what had she ever done that was brave? I hope you can now understand why I used that word.

Printed in Great Britain
by Amazon